I am my own self enemy and i am human

Nkosikhona Kwazi Qhaloshe

pencil

ISBN 978-93-5610-917-9
© Nkosikhona Kwazi Qhaloshe 2022
Published in India 2022 by Pencil

Contributors:
Illustrator: Zodumo Xalabile

A brand of
One Point Six Technologies Pvt. Ltd.
123, Building J2, Shram Seva Premises,
Wadala Truck Terminal, Wadala (E)
Mumbai 400037, Maharashtra, INDIA
E connect@thepencilapp.com
W www.thepencilapp.com

CONTENTS

Foreword

I would like to take this time and dedicate myself to telling the world about the struggle I have experienced in this book and about all the beautiful people I have got a chance to spend time with. I have included the names of some of the people but I would love to say that I dedicate it to someone who has influenced my life and how I see the world, she taught me how to live when I was merely existing, I caused her too much pain but I felt that pain I think even deeper than she did. she is the love of my life but I am willing to let the pain of losing her drive me to every height I can reach. if you've lived the life I have lived you would Know that great men I know took a certain amount of pain in order to rise up to being their true selves, I am talking about the Nelson Mandela's this world has seen, the Michael Jacksons, the Tupac shakurs and many more. I understand them and so to the love of my life Zodumo Zoe Xalabile I am greatly appreciative of your dedication to trying and make me a better man but I would also like to send a message to my grandmother wherever her soul rests "I love you and in my heart, you'll always live Magingqi omhle.

chapter one- my upbringing

I have been robbed of so much in my life and now I have hate-filled in my heart, I convince myself that I do not hate people, I just hate the world and how everything is designed. But the truth is that some of the events that caused me to develop this hate involved people. I for one am not perfect in some of them, I had as much a part to play in them. To tell my story I will have to go back to my roots, to when I was born. I have been told that I was born in Durban, in a township hospital called Bhambayi, back in 1998. My parents were not married, it was the time of war in the place where I was born, but I never asked what war that was. As you can imagine, all men were expected to fight when it was war and women would be left home to look after the house, take care of the kids, and hope that no one comes for them. On the day I was born my father was in prison, I am guessing it had something to do with the struggle that was going on then. He tells me stories that he got out of prison in a matter of days after I was born and that he was so happy that he had a son, that he loved me, played with me, and did everything that fathers do with their little babies. The struggle was still going on and I had to be sent to my maternal grandmother in Port St Johns, Majola. Of course, I do not remember much about those days, which I think is normal for everyone not to remember anything about when they were infants. But I do have some memories of that time that are stuck in my mind until this day. The first of those memories, I was being bathed and I was in a room full of people whom I suppose were my family because of the warmth that I feel when I recall that moment, it was a rainy day and I remember it very well because I cried when I felt the soap in my eyes and some of it in my nose. The second memory was also on a rainy day, my aunt was washing clothes by hand somewhere across from me but in the same room. I was not crying or anything but whenever I think about that moment, I can feel my presence in it. There is a third memory of course, but in this one, I was now a toddler and there was no rain outside, I crawled my way into the little house at home that was used to set fire to cook when it was raining outside, I saw a snake and I grabbed it with my hands. I do not remember the reaction of the snake when I grabbed it because I was not aware of its danger, quickly, one of my uncles saw this dangerous object that I had picked as a toy and came to save me. I do not know what happened to the snake, in fact, I never asked anyone at home about any of these incidents, I figured they are mine and I do not think that others can remember them, with a little exception for the snake one. I like to recall these moments, especially when I am down, and they always lift my spirit up. I think of them in the following way: I was new in the world and had nothing, I knew nothing except to cry when I was hungry or needed a change of diaper and yet everybody around me loved me and could not get enough of me. To understand what I mean by the preceding sentence, think about seeing a child who has been in the world for less than a year, everybody cannot help but fall in love with that little creature and everybody wants to hold it if they are not scared of the parent. I once carried around me that type of atmosphere, but as I grew older, I lost connection to my little self and I am no longer vibrating at that frequency where everybody could not get enough of me. The subject of frequencies is not something that I want to talk about deeply in this book as it belongs to a different subject or rather "philosophy" I just used it to illustrate my understanding of the circumstances. Anyway, in those days after I was sent to my grandmother, I think my mother left me and went back to Durban with my father because two years later my mother gave birth to my little brother. My grandmother was a very busy lady back then, she was a widow, and she was on her own taking care of her 10 children, I was the eleventh, she also supported my mother because after giving birth to my little brother my mother got sick, and so did my little brother. I never asked how long my mother waited before she went back to my father after she had brought me home, but I am sure it was a very short time because even to this day I cannot sense her presence in my life, it's like she was never there, and the fact that my grandmother got me a nanny since she was busy running her business and could not take care of me by herself shows that I was motherless. My uncles and aunts were already old, but they could not take look after me because they were going to school during that time. Eventually, my mother came back with my little brother, but she was very sick, I do have a little memory of her. In 2002 my little brother died, and not long after that, my mother died too. I was only 4 years old and did not understand what was happening. My father attended both funerals "so I've had" but I can only remember my mother's, and I remember it because I was so excited that my father was coming, before that he used to call on my grandmother's phone and he would ask to talk to me, he would make all those promises that fathers make to their little kids about buying them toys and coming to get them. I followed him the whole time to my mother's funeral, there was a family friend who was a cameraman, he took pictures of me on that day seating in both my mother's and my little brother's graves, and now as I write this and thinking about those images my heart recalls that memory. Anyway, after my mother was buried, my father disappeared from me on that day even though I had initially hoped that he was there to get me and that we were going to leave together. If you were a child who never knew his biological parents but was always hearing that they were coming to get you, you would understand how I felt. You see, parents lie to us when we are little, in their defense they claim that they are protecting us from a cruel truth, but I think they are protecting themselves from the shame of appearing a failure. Those empty promises and lies we were told when we were young, our reaction to them left something of memory in our subconscious minds, which as we grow gets triggered by some events, and since we could not deal with it early, because those responsible did not understand the damage their lies would later cause, we cannot understand it when we are now old when it is shaping our behavior because we do not know how to connect with the root of the problem. With my mother gone, I now had one mother, my nanny, but I never called her mom, even my own mother I never called her mom, the only person I called mom was my grandmother and I think it's because everyone I grew up around called her mom. However, my nanny and I shared a very strong bond, when you have spent so much time with a person when you were little and you grow up taken care of by that person it gets to a point that when that person leaves, they leave a hole in your heart. I remember in the evenings when she would knock off, I would cry for her, even when I was 4 years old, she would still hide from me when she had to leave, and eventually we were separated when I started going to creche. For some reason, my grandmother thought I was old enough and no longer needed special that special care that my nanny provided and that my aunts would now take care of me. From the above story, you can see how much a little black kid was robbed of at a very young age before he could start fighting for himself. Life tried me before I could even stand up for myself, I was robbed of the opportunity to be held by both my parents right after birth, and I was robbed of living with my biological parents because of the struggle that resulted in me having to be sent home to my grandmom, I was robbed of my other when she passed away, but before that, I was robbed of my little brother whom I would have loved to grow up with, I was robbed of my father because after my mother's funeral I only heard from him a few times and he disappeared like he was never there, I was robbed of my nanny when my grandmother believed that I no longer needed her but before that, I was robbed of my grandmother when she could not look after me by herself. At this point, someone would say I complain too much and that I am not the only person whose parents were not there full time, but this is my story, and I am putting my feelings on paper, the people I mentioned were my people, I was brought in this world so that I could meet them and be around them because maybe the universe answered our needs at the same time, maybe they needed hope at that time something to smile about and I needed a family, people who would love and take care of me and so our destinies were intertwined. I did not get enough of them. I want my mother, I would love to know her better so that what I miss about her will be more than just her pretty face which I saw in her photos on our photo album, I want her to come back and hold me, I want her to hug me when I face challenges in my life, I want to remember the times when she breastfed me so that I can have a genuine smile about the fact that she loved me and she was proud of me, and that I was not a little mistake she made when she was not thinking straight. I want to go back to the moment when I was born and I want my father to be there, I want him to hold my mother's hand as she pushes, and right after my mother has given birth to me I want the nurses to wipe me and give me to my father, I want him to hold me with tears in his eyes and tell me that he loves me and he is proud of me, he must promise he is not a perfect man but he will try and for as long as he lives he will always be there with me. My grandmothers owe me a doubled debt, I want my nanny back, "no" she did not have the right to decide for me that I was old enough and no longer needed a nanny, it was my nanny not hers and we had a bond like she was my biological mother. The lady who was my nanny still lives and she moved on, she got married and she has two sons and somehow, we lost our bond. I mean we are still friendly to each other, but it is not the same as back when she was the closest thing I had to a mother. I also want my grandmother to be the one taking care of me if my mother could not do it herself, I was her grandson and I deserved her full attention just like I am sure she gave it to my mother and her siblings when they were young. I want all the people I mentioned back, and I want their love to fill my days. I know that the circumstances under which I was born partly caused whatever I have just complained about "but to you my people wherever you are I just wish I could get more of your love" I also know that there were many paths that you could have chosen when you were deciding my fate, both constructive and destructive but you chose this one and in your idea, it was the best because it was the best you could give, given the circumstances. I am greatly appreciative to you for your contribution, but I have a bone to pick with life. But what is life, why is it so cruel to some people and so kind to others? Did life intend to bring me here around all these beautiful people who loved me only to rob me of them? Was it all part of the plan or did it happens randomly, do I have a purpose in this life, and were those circumstances part of that purpose? To answer all these questions, I will have to quote the philosophy "perhaps everything is interpretation" how I interpret and relate to a situation I am building myself around that situation in a manner that is identical to my interpretation of it. I refuse to believe that because my father was not there when I was born I was unworthy of his love, I refuse to believe that because I was not raised by my biological parents I was illegitimate, I refuse to believe that because my mother and little brother died when I was young I was meant to be lonely in this life, I refuse to believe that, because my grandmom could not look after me by herself and got me a nanny who later left when I was old enough, that they didn't love me. I believe that everything that happened during that time was purposeful, it was all happening for a reason that whenever I feel lost in the wilderness of this world I could look back to my roots and connect with my purpose because there is a reason why that pain did not break me. My purpose is to promote hope, love, and justice. When I was shouting at my parents in the lines above, I was not shouting at them directly, I was talking to life itself because my parents are also victims of life. It was the life that was responsible for all the circumstances that we endured, not necessarily to break me but to make me feel it, feel life. I believe you must feel life somehow if you will live. It can be joy or pain, but the feeling is important and no matter how bad my circumstances may seem to the ordinary viewer and how sorry they may feel for me, as long as I do not lose connection with my purpose, as long as I commit to the moment no matter how painful it is, they will never know or see the beauty of what I am experiencing or feeling inside. The time of my life that I just spoke about came and passed and it is because of my attachment to those moments that I seek justice from the universe, and it is not that I have a negative relationship with life, but I cared about those moments, and it was not of my consent that they were taken away from me. Do I want to go back to being an infant? "Not at all" I just want to feel the Genuity of the love of everyone around me like I did back then.

chapter 2 my philosophical views

Chapter 2- my philosophical views

I am my own self-enemy and I am human. Everything that symbolizes beauty and freedom in my understanding has been used against me through a channel called greediness. Greediness may at first seem like a necessary emotion, but it should be within limits. I shouldn't allow my greediness to make me my own slave because what I am to myself is what I will be to the world. To explain the foregoing statement, I will quote Earl Nightingale: "your world and everything in it is a reflection of your own mental attitude towards yourself". I am a firm believer in that statement, by allowing myself to be enslaved by my own greed I am sending a direct message to the universe that I am a slave and that if anyone needs me as a slave, they can use me by appealing to my greediness. As a result, people with the means, ability, and desire to enslave me will come into my life, and I will not see that they are slave masters because they will satisfy my greediness. "But what is a slave and who is the real slave master in this passage?" a slave is anyone who seeks power and control over that which is beyond his control, it can be power and control over others, power, and control over another individual's freedom to choose in a romantic sense. Power and control over material wealth or even power over the competition. The real slave master here is a lack of control over one's own mind and greediness. I am my own biggest competitor, my whole life I have measured my performance and progress by a standard set by others who do not possess any likeness to me, a standard that has nothing to do with my spiritual, intellectual, and physical capabilities: the name of that standard is "perfection" or sometimes it is called "just like so and so". Since the dawn of time, humans tried to escape their current state of existence by imagining a perfect world, something that is believed to have been a major driver in building civilization as we know it today. Everything we see around us is a result of this tool of imagination that we possess as humans that is believed we inherited from our creator. In its constructive use imagination has enabled magnificent creations by humankind that add ease to life. Both greediness and imagination have played a huge role in putting us where we are today. It has also been said that civilization was built by free enterprise capitalism and that at some point capitalism failed and there was a need for government intervention in order to protect the interests of the people. Both the government and capitalism are systems, and all systems are comprised of individuals who each seek to fulfill their own selfish interests. To digress a little, by selfish interests I mean all my desires as a separate being are selfish, it does not matter if that desire is for the public good the fact that it will make me look good makes it selfish. The government and capitalism neither of them is perfect merely for the fact that they involve individuals. I am a human and I acknowledge that I live in an imperfect world. My world is imperfect not because it does not have the things that I need to survive but because my desires are wants and not needs and since they are wants, meaning that I have a choice whether to pursue them or not they are selfish. Selfishness is at the core of all human desires, and it is harmless provided it does not harm others in any way. Up to this point I have talked about greediness, imagination, and selfishness which are all necessary states of our being as humans. And capitalism and government are the systems we have established in order to build our world, needs, and wants which I define as basic necessities to enhance our lives. At first glance government and capitalism might seem like enemies to one another, that is true for a small-time enterpriser who views government taxies as hindering the growth of his/her business. But when we up the scales and zoom the picture fully government and capitalism are one and the same and together, they have strengthened if not given birth to a very evil concept called "marketing" this is not to imply that marketing is all evil, my use of the word evil is based on the inherent evil side of our humanity and of course to have an evil side I must also have a good side. In this context, however, I will refer to the evil side of marketing. The birth of marketing was leading the way to the triumph of human slavery, and it enabled the emergence of digital devices, we have tv sets in our homes to keep us engaged in the content that is decided for us, we carry smartphones in our pockets which we can use to get on social media and be bombarded by all types of media contents from brand marketing to politics, financial, history, even pornography and so on. My fantasies of a perfect world have been conceptualized into a tool called marketing and that tool is used to manipulate me. From the shows I watch on tv I am told which clothes to buy, the kind of a person I should be, the career I should follow (if there's even anything called a career) and the latest trend is that I can now date people from distance with the use of social media. Everything I do as a human is because of marketing, I am always waiting for the right time in order to start living my life and I often seem surprised when such time never comes. Marketing is very good in portraying a fantasy, that is the whole concept of marketing is "to create a fantasy and make it look real and attainable". The human mind is very fond of generalizing because that puts it at ease and as a result of my ignorance and generalization, I have a tendency of linking things together that are totally different and conclude that they mean one thing. I conclude that money, freedom, success, and happiness mean the same thing when they don't. I can have money and not be free, I can have freedom without money, happiness, and success, and vice versa. Another mistake I make is to completely associate money with power, and of course, there is some association but that is not all there is to power. Everything that symbolizes beauty in my mind has been used against me. Music, digital content, romance, clothes, freedom, money, happiness, success, etc. are all used against me for the purpose that it is known I see beauty in them, and the list is not limited here. Music for instance in ancient times was used to heighten the sense of awe during worship ceremonies and that was also marketing because ceremonies are more of cultural and religious practices and any exchange of ideas is marketing. Today marketing has found a channel through music to enslave my mind. Anything that is made for the purpose of making money is marketing, it can be music, digital content or whatever but especially music and digital content because they are the major creators of trends and after a trend has been established there is social media to sell it worldwide. I ought to be careful. Music today teaches me how to love, it tells me I should chase money, I should wear fashion, it sets goals for me that through ignorance I accept as mine and I am always surprised when I do not get any satisfaction after I have achieved any of these goals, it is always not enough. The unsatisfied characteristic of my human nature is the strength that has always been used in building civilization, coming up with different ideas to improve human life. But it is also my weakness, and it is through the weak part of it that I am made a slave, and again the weak part of it is inherent in my nature. One of the sides of my being that has given the power to marketing is my tendency as a human being to put other people's problems before mine because I am longing for that status of being a HERO. A very misleading term in my language because it is another standard that I measure myself by and yet it was not set by me. Regarding heroism, I live by the rules which society dictates but I have been blind to its dictatorship because marketing is a kind tyrant. From primary school to university, I have read books about heroes, and I have tried to live up to their standards. I did not choose to read those books they were dictated by the syllabus and government, and because of that heroism has been programmed in my mind and I am always looking and searching for opportunities to become a hero, as a result, anything that resonates with me, I want to post about it on social media or talk about it to other people and by so selling an idea to as many people so that I can be worshiped and followed. At first, this makes me feel better about myself but only for a while and after that, the little satisfaction wears away and I search for other opportunities because I am addicted to heroism and all this while I think I am in control, but I am not, and marketing is. I am offering my service for free to marketing and because what I do perpetuates a fantasy, I am the first believer of that fantasy, everyone will not buy what I sell until they see positive results from me, I work so hard trying to live up to the fantasy, but it is unattainable, so I become dissatisfied, angry and depressed, I commit suicide leaving a note behind blaming other people for not caring. How can anyone offer their help to a person who has it all figured out "but do I though"? really, I am a slave. My position as a human being sucks, most of the time I know what I must do but I do not do it because I always have to think first "how will it seem to other people?" George Benard Shaw once said "the secret of success is to offend the greatest number of people" if my offense is not unlawful meaning I stick within the limits of justice, not intentional meaning I do not go out just to offend people it cannot be evil. I have to do it to fulfill a selfish desire that has nothing to do with proving anything to the world or anyone else but myself. As a separate individual, I have my own story to tell no one can tell it better than I can. And to tell that story I rely on marketing for distribution, my ideology is closely related to marketing meaning that all that I think I know about myself at this point has been a result of seeing, hearing, feeling, and then interpreting. But I should not let the good side of anything blind me from seeing its inherent evil side. Everything that has to do with me as a human has some element of evil in it, but I try so hard to deny this part of my personality and as a result, it always haunts me because I am ignorant to it and therefore, I am incomplete. If I pay attention and try to understand it, I would be able to embrace it and use it constructively. My evil or destructive side is associated with overindulgence in things, it can be the overconsumption of food, overspending on alcohol, overindulgence in sex, or even obsession with relationships. These all do not make me weak they do not make me strong, but they make me human. I am not perfect, nor will I ever be, but I can try to balance the two sides of me sometimes. Romance: my life has been influenced by a girl and I acknowledge the fact that I would never be where I am today if I did not meet her. I have always been told not to give too much power to another person over me because it is a recipe for disaster and because the other person cannot think of me first without putting her own selfish desires before. But what if giving her power over me is my own selfish desire, I have empowered the government and businesses and I have given them power and control over me, but I am told not to give the same power to the one that I love. I have been told not to trust and I should search for ideas or information that contradicts my decision to trust. What is the irony here, is it not that I was programmed since I was a kid to put my trust in organized power than in spiritual power? Love is spiritual, it is powerful and can be men's ruler. Governments on the other hand are a representation of a demigod in my imagination and it ultimately manifests as an object of fear. I do not stand against what I have been told to believe and accept as the way life should be. But I can make a conscious choice regarding love, I am a slave of love as much as I am a slave to marketing and addicted to fantasy. The idea here is not to deny this side of my personality but to acknowledge it. One of my favorite motivational speakers Elliot Hulse said something that I found very profound, he said "knowledge is transformative in and of itself" I raise my awareness so that I can accept all my sides so that they do not haunt me because of my ignorance. Most of the literature has been put together by ancient philosophers and they did so no not because they understood the world better than anyone else, they did so because they recognized that life is rather too big not to tell their stories. Transformation and development of civilization are necessitated by those who live behind more than a mere memory of themselves, it can be a piece of writing or any idea one could think of, together all these have been combined into the progress of humanity. Control: I am addicted to control; I want to control every situation I am involved in and that seems to have given birth to a manipulative side of me. But for me to be manipulative I have first to be manipulated by my own desire to control. Manipulation has the power to make me see myself in control of something that is absolutely out of my control- I will use an example to illustrate this. Recently I was involved in a situation where I lost my girlfriend it was bad, I did everything, I cried I had panic attacks, and I tried to win her back all with no success. So, I took my mind off that entire situation, and it seemed I was making the right headway although every little thought of that situation seemed to still evoke fear in me. I approached another girl while I was drunk and at first, my intentions seemed real and good to her, she did not agree to my request of being my girl, but the situation was promising, mind you, I was drunk so my emotions were high and it got to a point where I started posting photos of her. That attitude of posting her photos was motivated by my burning desire to prove to the ex-girlfriend that I am happy, my world can crash down on me, but I can still build a new one even without her. To my surprise the plan worked like magic even though it was not a conscious plan at all, and not that I complained because I got out of that situation what I truly desired, I faced my fears and things fell into place I got my ex-girlfriend back. Now whether or not the situation is fully remedied is a story of another day. What happened here is that I sold myself as an idea of a happy man worthy to be a partner to any girl, that was marketing aggressive enough. But aggressiveness and desire to control can fool me and make me a victim of my own mental manipulation. Advertising a product is necessary at the initial stage but going forward the reputation should speak for itself. using economics jargon I would say "monopoly and monopsony" are proper ends to pursue in a romantic relationship, there should be one seller in the market and a single buyer. But these ends are justified only if there is no other marketing interference of any kind going forward except for the maintenance of reputation by both parties involved. Since I have borrowed some terms from economics, I want to also put capitalism in this context, often enough it has been said that capitalism favors voluntary cooperation but that does not mean voluntary cooperation is practiced in a capitalist society. I must be aware of how much damage marketing is capable of doing in my psychology, when I am being primed with ideas over and over that is another form of coercion and the only difference is that it is psychological as opposed to physical, but that is what makes it even more dangerous because I am unaware of the fact that I am coerced. The tyrannical side of everything is inherent in me as a human, it is necessary in order to protect my loved ones. I still need my girlfriend or wife to listen and do some if not all the things I order her to do for me to be content with the level of protection I give her and the same with my kids. Someone might feel entitled to say "it is not anyone's job to protect any other person" but they will not say the same thing about the police. They would probably back their argument with proper logic from their point of view and they might be right, but what is right to them might be left to me, there can also be some element of unanimity in our arguments. It is my job to protect my loved ones because I want them to see me as a hero and that is the value, I am willing to add to their lives, this is marketing in action because I am forcing an idea into their minds that they did not strive for. Since the dawn of civilization, men have strived to be heroes both of their own stories and the people around them and that is inherent in my DNA since I believe in Gods and worship them for love, wisdom, and protection. It seems fit that I should also try to contribute to these virtues. I am willing to go through every imaginable pain in order to paint a good picture of myself in the minds of my loved ones and all in the name of love for humanity. Although the heroic part is inherent in me marketing pushed the narrative further. The availability of content in word form and promotion and distribution of that content is necessitated by marketing, whatever idea whether it is the bible commandments or law governing the country, literature, and so forth is communicated to the people through marketing. What I am doing here ladies and gentlemen are exposing the wolf and all its capabilities both good and evil. And I want to emphasize the point that both these sides "good and evil" are inherent in my being. Goodness and evil define me, I am both a slave and master of my own mind- I hope this paradox captures my intention to show how connected everything is that seems not connected in distance. Evil, love, and competition: the spiritual side of my DNA is the most complicated part of my DNA, and mostly because most of what manifests in the physical may also be a result of the spiritual side. To this day science and religion are unanimous about what they call one source or God but to this day I do not know how to guard the evil side of my spirit constantly. Boredom is both the enemy and friend of humanity, depending on my level of boredom I can either embrace my boredom and work on my own ideology (except when I am working) or I can seek the company of others to exchange ideas. I advertise my life and ideology to the world because I am trying to influence it positively, though my ideology may sometimes be interpreted as pure evil from a perspective of normalcy I need to raise awareness of the fact that normal only means common practice and not the proper standard of any being. Perhaps if someone else was to put themselves in my position they would understand my perspective. I will never get into any form of the relationship if I am not willing to trust my partner. Trusting a person does not mean they will not make mistakes, but I tolerate them because it makes them human. Some of the tv shows I have watched portray cheating and blackmailing, thus creating a trend about cheating and blackmailing, the trend circulates and cheating and blackmailing are promoted as normal things to do and so I regard myself as normal so of course, I will do what normal people do. Marketing is the biggest competitor of individual thinking or even individual decision-making. Competition is not all evil because I would not be at my personal best if I did not have some element of competition in my mind. I am not saying that humans should compete among themselves I am just bringing light to the fact that competition is there within us whether we want to deny it or not. Loneliness: I always complain about being lonely and I view loneliness as a bad thing, and I do not embrace it. I know of two types of loneliness; the first type is the loneliness I feel when I am in the company of people who do not add value in my life (but what do I mean by "people who do not add value in my life"? this is a contradicting statement because everyone and everything I see adds value in my life or at least has a purpose and I will explain. I imagine meeting a person who drinks alcohol too much, I never see this person sober and whenever I see them I say inside "help me God not to ever become like this poor soul" because according to my ideology in life this person is lost, but neither am I in the right path because I am just as clueless as he is about life, this person adds value in me because seeing them gives me an idea and I think of a man I want to strive to become), the second type is that loneliness I feel when I am awake and alone. I should be using this time to think for myself, and not entertain any other men's ideological views but my own, I would call this "shutting my attention off from marketing". Even though I cannot control my mind entirely and will recall some of the ideas I have been exposed to before at least I am not currently being bombarded with any new ideas. I should not entertain phone and tv more than I should as they are the media of marketing and so is communicating with another person. But sometimes I should rely on marketing to escape loneliness, and this is justified because, in the end, I cannot live in solitude forever. When loneliness hits I long for the company of others so that we can exchange ideas, watch tv to see how people live and see all sorts of ideas or go on social media to catch up on gossip and maybe post photos of myself or view those of other people. This is not entirely wrong but when I become addicted to it and forget that pictures only represent the moments that they were captured and not any constant state of being it becomes wrong. I can be happy now and in the next two seconds be sad and depressed. Food: Food is a basic necessity of my being; it fulfills a function of eating which I need to survive. All I need to fulfill this function is just enough, if my stomach is not groaning or aching and I am not yawning I am fine. Taste aside, there are nutrients that are said to be found in the food that I eat, and it is said that they are good for my health, vitamins, protein, energy, and others. There have been so many improvements made by marketers in the food that I consume but I believe that most of what is said about these improvements is just a gimmick. Most of the food ads on tv, billboards, or even on social media emphasize taste. Food is advertised in a way that I develop an appetite for it. Of course, appetite is an important emotion of my being because I still need appetite in order to consume any form of food. But I question the fact that food should be advertised to appeal to my appetite and promote emotional eating. I am being told that I must eat in order to fulfill a craving and not hunger, even though appetite is a necessary emotion of my being or the desire to taste and consume it is still a weak emotion if it makes me long for another type of food when

I have just eaten another type. The manipulative side of marketing exploits my weak appetite by showing me food that looks beautiful that I even imagine myself eating that food to a point where that image is accepted by my unconscious brain so that whenever I smell or see anything that looks like the dish that I saw on the advert I am compelled to buy it. Proof of this is in the fact that nowadays I do not plant my garden I buy everything from the shops, this is not because my soil is not rich enough, but this is because nobody shows me an advertisement for farming a garden in a more appealing way with constant effort as in food marketing. Saying everything I see is psychological no matter how real it may seem would be a cliché. But I will be a cliché just to emphasize a point, a trick I borrowed from my very big enemy and a friend called marketing (as contradicting as that statement is) who would say and do anything to prove a point in the name of improving human lives. Marketing and its tendency to collect userdata or in its rawness "human psychology" information have found a way to manipulate my psychology. I hate that such powerful information should be in the hands of anyone because it is literally destroying the world, and I do not understand the wisdom that came into play in combining that information. I am aware of my tendency as a human to want to know more about the world around me but that does not mean I must be manipulated into doing things that I would rather not do. I refuse to believe that this form of coercion from my kind is justified. I should not be forced to eat based on appetite when I would rather eat to satisfy hunger. Is it even necessary that I eat every day because I woke up today and thought I should defy everything I have been told, I woke up at 07:00 am and it is now 19:52 as I am writing this passage, I haven't eaten and I do not even feel hungry so I am not going to eat just the same way I do not visit a doctor if I am not feeling any pain, I thought I should test a theory and see if I do not go to the kitchen and I do not look at food ads will I be compelled to eat? I am still doing fine. I mean surely if I can survive not seeing a doctor when I am not feeling any pain I can survive not eating when I am not feeling hungry. I define hunger as that state of my being when I am yawning, my stomach aching and groaning. I did not feel any of that today, and even if I am still going to feel it, surely, I can survive responding to it tomorrow just the same way as I survive feeling pain today but only seeing a doctor tomorrow. No, I am questioning everything that I have been told and believed blindly, what if vitamins, proteins, and all other food contents do not really exist, would it not be fitting that I am told they exist so that I should consume them based on want and not need, commit to a diet which in my opinion comprises of a collection of foods. I am no scientist, I never looked on a microscope for myself to see if any of these food contents really exist, I just believe what I am told is true. What if it is all psychological like everything else, I have been told? Stoicism warns me to eat only plain food, but today's philosophy of marketing tells me I must consume all food contents. If one man's perspective is false another man's perspective cannot be true because we view matters with different ideologies. I should not be bombarded with marketing ideas about which food I should eat, it is my human right to make my own choice freely based on my own ideology. Women and marketing: as a man, the opposite person to me is a woman. My understanding of the opposite gender is that your anger towards me is misdirected, I know for a fact that my girlfriend or my wife (any that I have) has an element of hate towards me, that element is a result or after effect of discrimination of your rights in the past when me and you were unequal. You have eventually fought that struggle with me by your side and you have won. After your triumph in that struggle, a concept called feminism was born which guarantees you 50/50 chances with me in every arena of life. Marketing has eventually sold you a fantasy of independence and with your vulnerability, you have accepted that fantasy as the truth. This was a mind game targeted at you so that you could search for pleasure and comfort and your pleasure has been conceptualized into every item that you can even think of purchasing. You have been stripped away from my leadership and companionship, I on the other hand have been stripped away from your power to make things happen. As a man I have ideas, but I depend on you for motivation and implementation of those ideas. You are my other half; I doubt if mother nature made a mistake by making us opposites. Without you I am incomplete. I miss your natural beauty and your kindness towards me which makes me want to be real every day. I do not want perfection I want to see all your scars both physical and spiritual. Your persecution was also my persecution, I myself was a slave and living under the rules that society dictated as I still am today. Today me and you are both slaves and yet we still fight one another, marketing has organized that you change the way you look and be obsessed with their products, it has organized that you go from one man to another in search of perfection by playing different fantasies in your mind, it has organized that you put money first in a relationship and not the spirit, it has organized that you do not treat me with the same courtesy you used to treat me with, it has organized that you divorce me and make our kids together suffer in the process, it has organized that you do not cook for me anymore, it has organized that you overconsume alcohol, it has organized that you flirt and even cheat with other man and make them view you as an object of sex. I do not blame you for any of this, for the same has been done to me. I and you will never be enemies. I know I have been violent towards you, I have raped and killed you, in my defense, I say I did it all because I love you. But the right answer would be that I did it because I hate you. I hate you because today I do not trust you, I hate you because today I have seen someone who looks better than you do, I hate you because you are not perfect, I hate you because my friends do not think you are beautiful. And this is all a crime against you, and I do it all because out of ignorance I do not understand how my mind and emotions work. I am never satisfied with you, so you have eventually tried everything to satisfy me, you have changed how you look, you have changed your mental attitude towards life and adopted that of marketing gurus, and you have given the power to the cosmetic industry to use their marketing skills against you by exploiting your weakness. I do not know if any of this gives you happiness and frees your soul. But if your soul is not free you should know that mine is also not free just as the prison warden is still a prisoner. My struggle and yours are one and the same, we can be victorious by consolidating power because we need a bigger stick to poke the bear that is marketing, and if we can poke the right spot often enough, the bear will be stripped away of its power and hold over us. Money and marketing: Money is a medium of exchange and I use it to buy goods in the market or even pay for services. Before money emerged in ancient times there was a barter system whereby people exchanged goods, but this form of exchange had a problem of double coincidence. You had to want what I give, and I had to want what you give for the exchange to take place. So, to overcome this issue money emerged and has evolved over the years into the currency money that we are currently using. But I am not going to dwell on that history because it will defeat my purpose. From the definition I gave about money, there is no doubt that money is very important, and he who has it is at least free from thinking about how to make ends meet tomorrow. My attachment to it though gives me problems. Since I was a little kid, my parents were using money to provide for our needs, I was watching and I have been conditioned to see money as a very important tool, and it really is. I have also been told contradicting stories about it, and some go like "you should go to school so that you can become a lawyer and earn a lot of money, or money is the root of all evil" I have brought myself by careful consideration to the understanding that money is no root of evil. Throughout this book I have talked about the evil inherent in me as a human being, therefore, it is fitting to conclude even in this case of money that evil is in me and not money. The ideas I have been told as I grew up about going to work so that I could have money have eventually conditioned me to put even more value on money than I should, I have put money first in most of my endeavors however, this attitude has not yielded me any admired results. Because my love for money makes me feel empty, it is not connected to my soul. I have set goals of making money so that I could buy nice cars, live in big mansions, have sex with supermodels, and go to New York. To this day I have not achieved any of these dreams, I do not even have R10 in my pocket as I am writing this passage. The reason I have not got any money or achieved any of my fantasies is that they are purposeless. I have come to learn that I should live a life of purpose, I do this by finding a course of life that is meaningful to me without worrying about how much money I will make out of it, or whether I am going to make money or not. I would have to commit to that course with my heart and soul and strive to find my truth. In my opinion, love for money is the real root of evil. Although I have talked about my previous conditioning to see money as an important necessity in the life of my parents this has done not much harm to me, but simply make me realize that money is important in my day and age. What made me fall in love with the idea of just making money has been American Hip Hop music videos, movies, and local tv shows that portray middle-class living. And recently, social media and YouTube where I am constantly being bombarded with ideas about making quick money on Forex, online businesses, eCommerce websites, you name it. These are all harmless from the point of view of those who are responsible for them, I mean they are just sharing their ideas which brought them where they are now in life and by so trying to inspire while also making big tons of money. However, the way all this is portrayed is so perfect that it captures my immediate attention, another strength of marketing of course. At this point, I want to explain that I do not blame marketers for their efforts and enthusiasm to try and advertise perfection because everybody wants to progress. I still want to go to New York; I still have my fantasies. But I have accepted reality because of the pain and emptiness that I felt when I was going all out for money. Being a lawyer would really give me purpose provided that I am not doing it just for money, but I have chosen it as an end that I will strive for, for my entire life, and accept that money will come as a byproduct of that course and not worry about what amount I will get. What I did not know about money before is that it is psychological as well, it is worth what somebody says it is worth, and with phenomena like inflation I really understood this psychological aspect of money. To explain this, I imagine the old days of the barter system. If I wanted a product, I had to exchange it for another product, and the product that I have lost would be the value that I gave for the product that I have received. But that concept does not apply to currency money, because if I buy a product with money now, I will have to use that money now or risk keeping it and it decreases in value due to inflation. If someone has the power to determine how much a certain bill of currency is worth rest assured that is psychology in play because that value can be manipulated anytime someone decides to steal or fail to monitor monetary policy. Even so, money is still important, and I must have it, but the idea is that I should not put too much value on it because no satisfaction will come of that. Basically, what makes money even more important is that the way the world that I live in has been organized around me has been to condition me to buy everything, every product that one can think of, even another man's thoughts. This is what differentiates money from the system of barter because in the barter system I exchanged my own goods for another man's goods. The danger of money comes from my tendency as a human to develop more love for money than for service. For this reason, I have robbed for money, I have stolen money, and I have lied and killed for money. But to try and put things into perspective, this love is not really love for money, although in some twisted minds it can be. I fall in love with the image of having more money, looking good in the public's eyes, buying nice things, or saying "affording". Spending without worry on everything, is another strength of marketing, exploiting my weakness because the image of having plenty is a very powerful image in my mind as a human being and this is because of the conditioning I have received. I literally forget about the purpose of life which in my opinion is to live and search for meaning, I get addicted to money to a point where I even forget that the little currency in my pocket is not real money, it is just a manifestation of somebody's idea into a paper, it is the idea in the minds of those who formulated it and so it is they who understand it better how it works. Because the reason I have killed and got depressed and been involved in all sorts of atrocious situations over money is that I do not understand how it works. But how can I understand, how can I keep my mind constantly when everything I see requires that I have money. Well, the way that money works is that I must perform a service that is meaningful to the people. There is no easier way of making money than performing a service that helps other people. Let me also give you an idea of making money, get a job you like and if you cannot find it perhaps get any job, save all the money you do not need when you have provided for your needs, use that money to start a farm whether it is livestock farming or vegetables, start small you do not have to start big, you can even start on your backyard. Sell your products to the people in your community, make sure your products grasp the attention of your customers and they satisfy them, do not try to compel them to buy your products by any aggressive marketing, the only marketing strategy you should use is to offer them fresh and affordable price products, and also try to display your products in an inviting manner. I guarantee you will fall in love with watching your business grow from bottom to top and your attention will be swayed away from money. Because when you put too much emphasis on the money you end up not using it in anything of value. I had an experience that proves the preceding statement, I was a recovering alcoholic, I could manage to stay sober for a year and more, but my problem was that I used to hoard money, in my mind there was no purpose for which I was saving and the first suggestion of drinking, maybe passing by a club and spotting the vibe I would be tempted and compelled to get in and I would spend all my savings in one or two days. The immediate danger in the story is loving mere money, and especially if I do not work for that money, I never really appreciate it. The message that I wish to convey to myself and to anyone reading this book is that while on the subject of money is that I as a human being must perform a service for my fellow beings to earn money, whether that service is evil or just is dependent first on my point of view about money and then from the point of view of anyone else that the service will affect. What I mean by this is that if I am performing a service that will eventually earn me money, my consideration of the people that my service will affect and how it will affect the will determine how those people will view the service that I offer, whether it is just or evil. Justice for anybody should never be compromised since every right that I have as a human my neighbor also has the same right. Justice is compromised when I force my neighbor to pay for a service she did not require, this form of service is called robbery. Nobody invites or wishes to be robbed, I provide that service forcefully without the consent of my neighbor because I must make money and I must make it now. I just highlighted another issue about money in this passage which is my IMPATIENCE with money. This impatience is not however unjustified, all day long tv is priming me to eat that burger, or social media is priming me to get that nice set of wheels, get that watch, and this goes on for days. The acceptance of these suggestions by my unconscious mind puts me in the position whereby I am not patient. It makes me want to go out once and get all these things, and this is the reason I sell my soul willingly. But let me not blame it all on marketing, what is another issue that I raised in this passage, test yourself if you were paying attention, and find the issue by yourself. [""] it is ignorance, and it is not something I am talking about for the first time in this book. My ignorance of things, in general, is very bad, EC. Riegel once said "the enemy of mankind is ignorance of the inherent money power in all of us" I ought to know better, books have been written about why people should not spend so much time focusing on marketing stuff, and parents have warned me against spending too much time on tv. Because whether tv, or social media they all show marketing content, and that is what it is all about today. The trend has also been created in interaction amongst humans, and a concept called word-of-mouth has been born for me to influence my neighbor. Fashion is even worse because by just looking and admiring how my neighbor is dressed, he will not even have to make an effort and talk about his clothes, no I will as for myself, "where did you get it?" and not just fashion but anything that is sold. Marketing is very effortless these days, any new product is just posted on social media, and maybe get a celebrity shows it in his music video and the rest will happen on its own, I like Cassper Nyovest so I will share his video on Whatsapp or Facebook so that my friends can know which type of music I listen to and who is my favorite artist. What I may not realize is that one of my friends might see a t-shirt on that video, that bottle of Ciroc and another one might see that BMW and that sexy model. This is all marketing my friend, it has been made for the purpose of making money and getting customer loyalty. Now to have the things I see I need money, right. Imagine I was saving some money, maybe R100 every month and I am up to R700 now. Will I not be compelled to buy that t-shirt if I love it even if it is not the purpose for which I was saving. Marketing is an enemy of money because it gets me swayed from the purpose, I was saving for and compels me to buy something now that I was not planning to purchase, and that concept is called impulse buying. This is important if you are reading this book, I need you to pay attention, you would not save money if you did not have a purpose for it (I know the story I told about purposeless saving and being a recovering alcoholic, but that story was only valid to defend my stupidity), maybe your early retirement. But now at the first glance of something I love that is being marketed or promoted I spend my money without even considering it. am I not going to be a puppet that gets pushed around by marketing? No, this has gone too far now, I live a purposeful life and everything that I do must be according to my purpose. If I want a t-shirt, I will recognize a need from within for it, but I am not going to buy it because I see it and I have money, I will not just see it and then be pushed around to go and look for the money so that I can buy it. I will not buy it because it makes me look good to society or other people's eyes, no I will take my own advice, my need will come from within, I really will not be pushed around like a puppet by a wolf seating on the couch and watching me while I self-destruct, that wolf called marketing. I even ask myself a question if the people who first introduced marketing, those who conceptualized it and made it what it is today, are they still able to control it, or have they created a monster that even they are now not able to control, can it happen that even they believe in the fantasy now and are slaves like I am, can it happen that when churches talk about the evil that shall come they are talking about the evil that we bring to ourselves and then lose control of it? Because when I think about all the things I have talked about in this passage, which are money, cars, fashion, and marketing. They were all introduced first because they were needed, everything gains power as the need for it by humans becomes intensified. Money too has become a very powerful tool and is used for all good and evil purposes. Money gained its power, not from the fact that it is so important on its own, no because if it was so important on its own our central banks would print those papers very cheaply and distribute them wherever they are needed. What makes money important is the psychology behind it, I want to emphasize this. If I have been told since I was a little kid to chase money, because life without money is meaningless or difficult and I cannot be seen as a respected member of society if I do not have money, think of the effect that would have on my psychology. The first thing it would do is it would instill fear in me whenever I think about not having enough which on its own is an unnecessary thought to be entertained by any individual. Often times when I am thinking about money I am not even thinking about the present, I am thinking about the future. I always worry about "if I don't save enough now, who's going to feed me when I retire". Money is not meant to be hoarded, it is a means to purchase our current needs and a need in the future should not be my concern I do not even know for sure if such time will come for me, I am only promised the present. This is not to say that I will not save, what I mean is that I will not overspend on useless things that I do not need, and I will also not hoard while I suffer, whatever I can manage to save when I have been taken care of will do me just fine. I will do now what I plan to do in the future. I believe that if there is a future and I will be in it then I will be okay without worrying now. What I will need in the future will be provided when the time comes. I think about where I am right now in university, and I have all that I need, at some point in my life I never even thought about being here, but I came just fine. Time has provided for me to have the things that I need to exist in this environment. If time provided me now, then I believe that the time in the future is still a capable provider. But the problem about me as a human is that I spend half if not most of my life worrying about what will happen if so and so happens in the future and this makes me focus on the future and be completely ignorant of the fact that I can only control what I do now. This is the same attitude towards saving many, I worry about not having enough in the future or ending up being homeless and becoming a laughingstock to society. These all have nothing to do with my spirit because my spirit can only be where I am now. Even now I do not have money every day and I receive it once a month, but I am still able to make ends meet and save the remainder. I must not be attached to my savings, by keep checking them every day is another form of love for money, and that might make me end up reading books about making more money, those books do not help me if they make me lose myself and start buying everything they sell. I once listened to a guy saying "if you want to make more money you should spend fearlessly and then call it to come by thinking about it" that was his perspective and for him it was right. The response in my mind was that "if I have to think about it and call it to come" then that is love for money and not the purpose, and "fearlessly" in my mind sounded like impulse spending. One of the reasons I love money today is because I spend too much buying what I want and not what I need. What I mean by that is that of course, I need transportation, but if public transportation is cheaper than having my own car then buying a car would mean that I am buying it to satisfy a want. I know there are so many advantages of having my own car and they probably outweigh those of using public transport. But the message I am trying to convey here is that what is in the best interest of me as a consumer of a need is to buy it cheaply. This story of need and want can cause a huge debate in the mind of a person reading it but the point of the story is merely to bring light to the fact that my tendency to spend on what I want as opposed to what I need has also contributed to my love for money. This money love is also caused by seeing people who have plenty and the things they buy. The pain in all of this is that putting money first makes me lose connection to who I am, if I want it because my neighbor has it, I am abandoning my own individuality and trying to be somebody else, I fake a life that is not really mine because money is that important in my mind. Most of this passage about money may sound like I am putting all the blame to external factors, but I must agree that the desire to have plenty comes from within and the way it is so powerful I will assume that it comes from the spirit, my spirit loves beauty, and it seems to be always seeking expression through nicer things but I am confused whether there is a way I must control that spirit, maybe this is all because of previous conditioning. I think I must decide which channel I will direct my spirit, to pursue money directly or to strive to offer a service and have no intense attachment to the money. My choice is the second one, a service gives me purpose and it keeps my mind engaged on something else than money. What I think my spirit needs is not necessarily money or nice things that money can buy. What I think my spirit needs is for me to direct it toward a specific point, and believe me, I have once in my life made that point about money as I said before. It was not good, I do not want to speak for any other individual, it can be that just making money was not my own purpose in life but somebody else's. It is the service that gives my life purpose and not money in its raw form. The way marketing perpetuates a lie about this object of money makes me wonder if anyone out there, maybe their destiny is not so different from mine, but they chose the wrong course of life. Because if I am not engineered to just make money then it must also be that there is someone else out there who also is not.

Pornography: I was addicted to pornography very recently in 2019 but I want to start this story with a little background. When I was a kid around my 8-10 years, we had a tv at home. My parents would go to sleep early, I and my neighborhood friends would stay and watch tv almost all night on Friday and Saturday nights. At midnight on those 2 days, there was a show that used to play on Etv. The show was called blue movie and it was a porn show. We would watch this show me and my friends, and we did not even know anything about girls back then, neither of us even had a girlfriend during that time. But we would watch the show nonetheless and we would be sexually aroused, and we enjoyed the feeling otherwise we would not watch it if we did not enjoy it. That show, however, ended and I think it was in violation of the revised code of conduct in my opinion. And we stopped watching porn when it ended. By the time I went to high school, I started having girls and sex and I started watching porn videos to see positions, this time not in the company of any friends. But I was in control during that time I only watched briefly maybe once or twice a month, I would even forget that even had them. The trouble started when I got to university in 2019, the first thing I got when I got here is a laptop and I was living a in student's accommodation with an uncapped Wi-Fi connection, and I was free to browse the internet without worrying about data. What happened is that I loved watching movies and listening to music, and

I still love them even today. Here in South Africa, we have free sites to download music and movies, but what I did not realize in the beginning is that free is not free. It does not make any logical sense why something someone is selling, somebody else can give it for free. When someone says something is for free what they actually mean is that you do not pay money directly, but you will pay another way. In those free movie sites as soon as you are in, you are bombarded with all pornographic content, links to play sex videos, links to dating sites, and even links to casual sex meetup sites. And you get these suggestions the whole time you are in there, they keep popping up and some finally catch your attention, and you start viewing them. One minute you spend viewing any one of them is very dangerous because you get hooked to stay. The display is flawless. I did all that, I viewed videos when no one was watching me. I started seeing what those people are doing as perfect sex, and they fueled my sex drive, okay maybe I am lying a bit because as I remember my sex drive was always high. But what they did I became so obsessed with sex to a point whereby I would lose focus on my studies because of a burning desire to watch porn. I became a porn addict, and this was during my first year at university. I was getting afraid because I was at a point now where I could not hold myself towards porn. During this time my girlfriend was in Cape town, and we were 1000s of km apart, so I was not getting any help from anyone. What really got me started in this was being bombarded with this view of perfect sex. I would see all these white women naked and as a black guy, I would say to myself "if I could have sex with them, it would be perfect" At that time I would have easily sold myself to the porn industry if there was an offer because I was so obsessed, and it was very bad. I followed links to casual sex sites, and I spent money on those sites buying credits, but those credits were not real because I was never able to chat with anyone, I kept being told to upgrade from one premium to another and I thought they were crazy. I was at a point where I needed to change, no I had to change. I told myself I would force myself to change, but when something has been conditioned in my mind it takes effort and mental strength to overcome it. I started little, I fought that urge for a day and succeeded. On the second day, I did it again but on the third day, I would have a relapse. Sometimes I would relapse for two or even three days in a row, but I would fight again another day. It is very difficult to fight something that has become a habit. It was like it was happening unconsciously, but the truth is that I was aware when it happens, but I would just let it drive me. I remember I had more than three failed attempts to fight this before I could succeed. I realized that I was winning but allow myself to fall back and I was at a point where it felt like I was losing resistance. So, what I did is that I told myself I would start the fight again, first I looked at my two roommates at that time and they looked fine and were not hooked in of this. They just loved politics and they did not even know while I looked normal on the outside, I was dying inside "but how would they know" it is not like I would let them see me watching. Anyway, made me realize that I had to fight to get my life back and I was going to fight relentlessly. I made up my mind that I was not going to be controlled by something that I started by myself, on top of that a habit that I was not born with. What I did is that I would win the first day and then apply the same attitude to the following day. In this attitude, I did not try to fight my mind from trying to give these suggestions to watch porn and I would not even try to shut down my emotions, I would just let everything happen knowing that as long as the porn will not play itself then I am not going to do it. This attitude kept me going until I was in a state where I felt like I have succeeded, but while in that state what I realized was that when I went to download a movie I would be wooed by those ads, and I would sometimes start viewing then stop by fighting myself actively. This made me realize that the fight was not over yet. It was now time for me to focus more on my studies. I would read but when I am chilling, I would still watch movies, I would still go to my sites but this time I was not paying attention like before because I was aware of what could happen, I would look at the porn ads popping up, but I would not browse any. The finishing of the story was something of a miracle, I eventually won that fight, and the way I won it I was not even fighting it anymore. I reached a point where I was interested in making a lot of money, something else that was suggested to me when I downloaded movies on my sites. People were advertising stuff like "how to make a million in one day" then I went to google and search for ideas on how to make money online, and I picked the idea of affiliate marketing, mind you another recipe for disaster because I was all about making money, which I have explained in the previous chapter. My mind got engaged in another area yet another disaster. I was learning how to build an affiliate website from a free online course, I was seemingly making the right headway, but I never made even a cent. I spent more than three months trying to figure this out. All this time my attention was completely consumed by this thing, and I had forgotten about porn. When I eventually failed in this idea, I searched for books that talk about making money and I found Napoleon Hill's THINK AND GROW RICH. I could only read-only Two pages and I stopped because I had no disciple for it, my goal was to make money not to read any other book when I had enough of my schoolbooks. But I kept that pdf on my laptop, and I kept that affiliate marketing idea in my mind and postponed it for the following year. I failed again the following year, then I decided it was time to move on. I fell in love with reading my books, I even read and finished THINK AND GROW RICH four times. That is the book that got me started in philosophy, from there I watched Bob Proctor's seminars; the born rich program where he fully explains how the mind works. From there I knew I had won the battle against pornography even though I was no longer fighting it consciously. I was now understanding how what happened to me and why did I change. I am not going to dwell on THING AND GROW RICH here as there is a free pdf available online for free download, I am also not going to talk about Bob Proctor's born rich series of seminars because it is available on YouTube, I was only making reference to what really helped me change. Now back to business, what does the term pornography mean? If you go to google you will find the definition of pornography as; printed or visual material containing the explicit description or display of sexual organs or activity, intended to stimulate sexual excitement. From this definition you can tell this is marketing, I did not even have to try and link the two terms they are the same. In my point of view, the pornography industry is not unaware of the serious damage that pornography is capable of doing that is why they pay more money on free sites to advertise their content and they make a lot of money too. This is not illegal because they are not ruining anyone's rights. They like any other business are just selling a product. From the story I just gave you can see that my love for movies and my unwillingness to pay for them is what got me in trouble. Those free sites are "enter at your own risk" sites, no one can hold them liable for anything. I would say I did it to myself because by downloading movies for free I am hurting another business; I do not give them value in return for their product and by doing so disobeying the very law of nature which is to give equal value for that which you get so pornography must have been karma. But I do not want to get into the spiritual side of things. If I want movies if must pay for them, free movies are not really free. Sex is a biological human activity; it is also the most powerful emotion of my being. I do not like the fact that it is advertised carelessly like that. But of course, there is a market for it so was necessary that the product must be made available. The truth is I am different, and you are also different, you want sex to be displayed and I do not. but whose right is put above the other here because I also did not choose to see those ads? This is just like any other form of advertising I did not choose; it can be food or anything. The truth that I wish to convey here is that what helped me here and what continues to help me today is discipline, but before I could have discipline, I had to understand how it works. Out of many things that could have made me enslave myself to pornography, one that is so manifest is ignorance. This was not the first time that ignorance had made me pay dearly. I am aware of the fact that movies are sold so that actors can get paid. But when I discovered that there are sites where I can get movies for free, I did not stop to think that there must be some hidden agenda here because you cannot have somebody selling their product competing with someone who is giving it away for free. My conclusion in all of this after I had suffered and eventually won was that the movie makers who sell their movies for money also had some sort of a relationship with the porn industry and that they gave consent to their movies to be downloaded for free so that the porn industry can make money and pay them handsomely for distributing their movies. This made sense back then, it still makes sense today. Out of all things that could have saved me I think the first best step that I took was a revolt that I affirmed to myself from within, that "I had to stop" this led me into taking steps that I would not tell initially that they would make me succeed. I think there was also an element of faith even though I was unconscious of it because now come to understand that you cannot start to do anything unless you have faith that you can succeed. I freed myself from slavery, I was more a slave to my own ignorance than to pornography. I had to disobey my emotions and deny my mind pleasure in order to be freed. Every slave must free themselves, if you are reading this passage and you can relate to what I have just said or you are currently going through the same thing, I wish to tell you that only you can free your soul. Ask yourself why am I doing this and then examine whether the why is worth the pain that comes with addiction. I believe I can win any fight with the attitude that I used in my fight against porn. But if not everybody then you have to find your own strength, but it has to start with you rebelling against your own desire for pleasure. Social Media: social media is a very powerful tool marketers have at their disposal, they use it to advertise their products, sell products, and even get reviews from customers. This powerful tool is enabled by the internet, and it is not only limited to marketers but everyone with a supported device can access it. social media has changed the way people communicate with each other, how they consume content, and engage with their favorite brands. In this very powerful tool, there are so many options for which content to subscribe to, and in the beginning customers or users really had a choice. But I cannot say the same thing about today. Previously, social media sites were more of a communication tool than marketing, until marketers saw an opportunity to advertise their products. When social media was still only a communication tool or maybe when marketing was not as aggressive as it is today, I was able to communicate with my loved ones without worrying about airtime since it uses data and data that lasts more than a phone call. This was amazing back then; I could engage in a conversation with a few people and even go really deep. But marketers realized how powerful social media is and they started advertising their products. This enabled social media platforms like Facebook, Twitter, and WhatsApp to add more features so that businesses can successfully advertise their products. These features however are not only limited to the use of marketers. These are features like posting a status, sharing photos and videos, and users can even share some of the content they like on their timelines so that it can be viewed by their friends, I would call this word of mouth except it is digital. Through all of these marketers do not have to make much effort to advertise their products. They just have to get it on social media and there is even a tool that enables them to target specific demographic groups and locations that have shown interest in similar products before. This specific targeting is enabled by another tool that these platforms have an algorithm that collects user data. Up to now, social media marketing has become too powerful. This is because the number of users increases every month, and people are charmed by the thing these platforms can do. For example, on Facebook, you can post a photo and other users will react and comment on that photo. This gives users satisfaction and a feeling of worthiness in the beginning, and it keeps you engaged in the platform. I remember when I started using Facebook, I would post a photo and I would keep checking after every two minutes if other users have reacted and how many are they. This was hurting my psychology because often times I would see no change and I would feel worthless. I would feel like people did not like me. This attitude is common to people who are new to these tools, they really pay attention to reactions and numbers of viewers, and even those who have been using these tools for a very long time still have this attitude because it has become a habit. It is not uncommon to see someone eating food while they have their phone on the table scrolling down their newsfeeds. What I realized on my side is that while I was so obsessed about the number of likes I was getting, and I kept viewing them when I logged in what appeared was only my photo. I would see what other users are posting and what businesses are marketing. I would see products that I love, products that some of them I had never seen or heard of them before. I would also see people that I did not know, and I would sometimes view their profiles and find that we live in the same town or close. The truth is that social media raised my awareness of so many things and I believe that it is a very good tool. I had increased awareness of brands, people, jobs, really everything anyone could think of, and back then you would really choose which content you want to subscribe to, and you would actively search for people you want to see and communicate with. I was even introduced to social media dating, something that I owe a big thank you to because that is how I found the love of my life. But today the story is not the same. Things have changed. There is no privacy at all on social media, especially on Facebook. I see contents that I did not subscribe to every single day. Some of the content I never even subscribed to was similar content before, and this is all because someone has decided what they think is best for me. Of course, I am curious about what is out there but that does not mean that ideas should be forced on me. Even more, features have been added today, and people can even go live on these platforms. But what I have noticed is that Facebook is more of a marketing tool today than a communication platform because as soon as you start a conversation with anyone they answer briefly, and I can see that they are still online, but they reply late. This is not necessarily because they do not want to talk to me, they get swayed by this marketing content and get engaged at a different level. No one can blame them; it may seem that they are practicing their right by doing what they want. But not every one of them even knows what they are doing, some of them have no choice, they just see themselves engaged in this content and they do not know how to prevent it. You say no one is forcing them "that is not true" anyone who understands psychology and knows what priming is and how powerful it can be would know that these people really have no choice. What this is doing is that it hurts relationships whether it is romantic relationships, family, or even friendships. Because when I text you and I see that you are online I expect you to reply with the same enthusiasm you show when we talk in person. This is really bad, especially for people who do not really know what is happening. Of course, there are still some contents that I subscribe to, but who gave anyone the right to also share similar content at the same time. Someone might say on tv you watch generations, but you still see the ads. This is different because on tv I did not open an account and give my details. I understand there are people who condone this attitude on social media platforms, it is because of them that this attitude was even formed. Marketers hide behind statements like "we want to reach as many people as possible we can but accept any number of engagements we can get" but on platforms like Facebook where everyone scrolls down their newsfeeds this is wrong. Priming my mind with media content is another form of coercion. Because even though some of us are aware of what is happening, there are those who are not aware. This is some twisted form of the "no one size fits all" approach. In the matter of posting photos, which also has an element of breaking relationships, what I have come to understand is that people view and do things differently. If for example I am in a relationship with a girl and she posts a photo of herself and people start reacting and commenting, what I have come to realize is that I would go to her comments section and see who commented and what did they say. This is all an illusion because first of all men out there are perverts, myself included. We have accepted this image of women as sexual objects. So, in that comment section I will see all sorts of "I love you, babe, my favorite" really any stupid thing any loser could think of to call your girl and you blame it on her. If anything, I should support her because this is harassment. What I am trying to say is that social media has also made us not to trust, and I believe that a romantic relationship is spiritual and there will be a change in the energy If there is an element of mistrust. But then again, I want to take attention away from the platform and brink it inwardly. What I have learned is that what happens on the outside does not necessarily determine what happens on the inside. Relationships before social media were a matter of faith and truth. You trust your partner because you have faith in love. If my partner has told me she loves me, and she has not taken it back I have no reason to doubt her. If there is anything to be seen I will see it but that does not mean I should go and spy on her comment section because I might find what I am looking for, and also what I find might not be necessarily true. What I have been doing throughout this book is exposing the bad sides of the topics that I have talked about and then bringing light to the fact that people themselves are not helpless in the situation. In the matter of marketing content and the psychological effect of priming, it is just a matter of raising awareness. When people are aware of what is happening, they are not helpless because they can take action anytime, they make up their minds. Because the truth of the matter is that even if these tools have negative sides, they still have positive sides, and they are needed because they make life easier in some way. What I can say for myself is that my awareness of all of these has given me an edge. I am at a point where I am not worried about controlling the tools themselves. I just control myself. If awareness gave me that power, I am sure it can do the same for you. Alcohol and marketing: Alcohol is a very destructive tool that can be used to destroy mankind. The way it is advertised is very deceiving, you never see its destructive nature in the ads, but that is the whole concept of marketing, to focus on the positive factors. I do not know if there are positive factors about alcohol, but the way it is marketed portrays the image that it makes it easy to socialize and they associate it with all sorts of feelings that humans long for; power, success, pleasure, and having a good time. Really all sorts of things. When I see an advert for brandy on tv and they are drinking it in a boardroom my mind concludes that a successful man drinks brandy because I do not know about the whole concept of selling an image, I am just a rural boy who aspires to be successful. Rich men are not really targets of these liquor brands, it is the poor people who have these fantasies of having power, and being in a boardroom, and rich men do not need to aspire to that because they are already living that life. I do not know if it is psychologically proven that when the human mind sees a certain brand associated with a certain feeling whether it is success or pleasure, it concludes that they mean the same thing. But I know from experience that it happens. The concept of focusing on the positive aspects of a product is a root cause of the harm that these products cause to consumers. I am told on ads that alcohol gives me pleasure, and of course, there is always I little note that is written saying that I should drink responsibly, but no one puts emphasis on that as they emphasize the part about fun. The fact that people are not informed about the destructive side of alcohol is a question that should be addressed. Marketers should trust their customers with that information. The fact that some information is withheld raises concern, are we being destroyed on purpose because that is disloyalty. No one tells me that alcohol is addictive the way they tell me that I will have fun. Seeing only a note on the wall of some nightclub saying alcohol is addictive seems like some twisted form of reverse psychology. It does not suggest anything, I believe there should be ads showing what addiction looks like. One can say that movies do that, but movies do not focus on one specific point, and they do not keep appearing in the public's eyes like ads, and movies also have an element of promotion in them as well. They promote these brands. As a human, I have both constructive and destructive sides and I live well by maintaining the balance between the two sides. Being informed about both constructive and destructive use of the product does not necessarily mean that I will stop consuming it, it will help me find a way to balance them. I live in a country where youth is on self-destruct mode. We were not always like that, we did not always consume alcohol the way we do today, and we did not always make it about pleasure. It is just that the media has succeeded in putting that image in our minds, we have been programmed to believe that alcohol will give us pleasure and that we should always seek pleasure. The way our nightclubs have been designed and how people socialize is another adding factor. Nightclub owners only saw an opportunity to get a piece of the pie, the masterminds of the game are the brand owners. They have placed an image in our minds for years and it is stuck there like a lamp on a post, it determines where we should go for pleasure, and how we should socialize. I do not deny the fact that these are possible states that alcohol can cause, but we do not depend on it to have fun or to socialize, we have always been able to do so. What this image has done is make us not believe in our own capabilities to bring about these states. A clear example is that of a brandy being advertised by men in a boardroom, of course, that image will emphasize calming the nerves and boosting confidence. An individual who is doubting themselves will see this as a remedy to his problem. The marketing of alcohol today is very powerful, especially with the emergence of slay queens. Every man drools for slay queens and placing them in the image of liquor also contributes to why most men cheat on their wives when they are drunk. They go to the club with the desire to see slay queens and so they must get them. An image that has been repeated over and over in one's eyes becomes accepted by his mind, and it becomes his truth. It becomes very difficult to overcome that image. You hear men saying they want to quit drinking, but they cannot because in their minds drinking gives them pleasure or a feeling of success. Maybe it does but I want to inform you that the major contributing factor to that belief is the fact that you have been programmed to believe that it does and whatever feeling you get when you drink your mind will conclude that it is pleasure. I have my own story of how destructive alcohol can be in one's life and as much as I am fond of saying that as a human I have power, in fact even on this matter I do believe that I have power, but only here the battle is huge because first of all pleasure, fun, success, and power are some of the sates that humans have been in pursuit of since the dawn of time. They give one a sense of satisfaction. Associating these states to alcohol, one of the most powerful brain stimulants is an unfair fight against consumers because by placing an image in my mind and I have an experience of drinking, recalling that image forces the blood to recall the feeling I get when I am drinking in that setting. Now I have to fight against my own mind and emotions. This is the type of information that marketers should also distribute to consumers, not this media propaganda they are selling. I thought my own experience would be a fitting climax to put things in perspective and show how destructive alcohol can be.

Chapter 3- Alcohol nearly destroyed my life.

Having fun: alcohol is one of the most if not the most consumed products of our generation. This is because of so many reasons. People drink for fun, to escape boredom, to relieve stress, to calm nerves before an important engagement, to socialize, really, so many reasons. I do not know what my reason was, but I have drunk alcohol and I have had fun in my life. I had my first drink on 25 December 2009, but I was only experimenting I was still a kid, and I was only 11 years old. I and my friends rebelled against our parents, in fact, we did not even rebel because they never found out where we were and what we were doing. Saying we rebelled in the above statement only means we rebelled against their warnings and teachings which they had given us ever since we were little kids. This did not cause any problems we did not feel any after-effect, like getting drunk because we were drinking 3 beers and it was more than 8 of us. It was not only me and my closest friends but more like many other kids in the area where I grew up. I grew up in a small rural settlement called Lupapasi in a very small town called Port St Johns which is located in the Eastern Cape province. We did have fun me and my friends that Christmas. Back then the tavern was new in our location, and it was still one of those peaceful times when everybody showed love and you would barely see people fighting. We were still very young and very underage to be even drinking, let alone being in a tavern, and to even get the beers we were drinking we would ask the older guys that we knew we were cool and would have no problems buying for us. Neither of us even enjoyed the sour taste of beer on that day, I remember my sip back then was not even half long as recently. What gave us fun that day was the music and seeing other people. Especially if you grow up in a rural settlement, in December many people come from their workplaces to visit their parents and relatives. There were many new faces that day even our peers who lived in big cities like Durban, and Joburg would come around and we would make new friends. Well, back then we believed they lived in the city because we were too young to know the reality that they actually lived in the townships, some of which our rural settlements are way better than them both in safety and quality of life. But like I said we did not know any of this, so my friends and I were charmed by these guys. We would listen to them telling stories about where they lived, the kind of life they lived, about their beautiful girlfriends, really all kids bullshit. It was really fun; I remember we even watched older guys who were kissing their girlfriends and we would also go after girls our age when we saw them on the way because we were not really stuck in one place. Not that we had any experience with girls, but we were just fooling around, and we enjoyed it. Until this day I miss those days. Childhood memories are worth more than a million to me. This behavior did not make us wild kids or anything like that and the money we used to buy beer was given to us by our parents. Where I grew up, parents would buy new clothes for their kids for Christmas, and they would also give them money not only parents, but uncles also gave us money. In fact, everyone on that day used to open their hearts, especially to kids. We finished our beer and fooled around chasing girls and we did not even know what we were going to say to those girls we were just fooling around, and they also ran. Everyone had that Christmas spirit. Late around 6 pm-7 pm, we would all go to our homes because parents did not want their kids out of the yard when it was late. I got home and I was welcomed with a delicious Christmas meal. My grandmother, my aunt ["bless their souls"] and everyone who was home when I got there did not even detect that I had a drink. Not that they could have, I mean we did not only drink beer that day. The tavern was near a shop, and we bought snacks and cold drinks, beer was just for experimental purposes. We continued this behavior again the following December in 2010. We would not do anything during the year because we were not really drinkers, we were just kids, and we would engage in school during the year. And also, in my location, the tavern would only get busy in December and on Good Friday weekend. You would find some small busyness on paydays when elders were collecting their pensions. In 2010 however, things had changed. People from my hood were now used to that life and were now acting like hooligans. People would get stabbed and even die. So, we did not have any fun that Christmas. Even at home, the atmosphere was down because, in small rural settlements like mine, when the youth are killing one another, all parents fear for their own kids. That December I stopped fooling around. Until 2015 when I started to drink officially. I became a consumer. I was doing grade 11 at Port St Johns Senior Secondary School. An uncle of mine who was working in Cape Town during that time was back home, and I was living around town. He called this other day; it was on Friday, and he told me he was in town. I was so happy, and I did not even know that he was back from cape Town. School was already over that day, and I was also planning to go home for the weekend but when he called, I was still in my room at the place that my grandmother was renting for me. I had already packed my bag with my uniform so that I could wash my uniform when I got home, and I had also in my bag some clothes that I was going to change with when I got home because I did not have any clothes left at home all my clothes were with me where I stayed, and I would carry some with me when I visit home on weekends. I took my bag and went straight to town, and I met my uncle. We looked around town and when I met him, he was already with my cousin sister who was also going to my school, and we lived in the same place. We went around with my uncle, and he bought the things that he wanted to buy, and he took us to KFC, we had our meal and then he said he would like a beer and he asked if I was drinking. I left a detail because in 2014 on the 16 of April I had a drink with my high school friends and I got really drunk, we were going home for Good Friday so there was going to be a small 10-day holiday. So, when my uncle asked if I drink, I was tempted and I said yes right on the spot. He asked what I would like to drink and of course, the first instinct would be something sweet that would also make me look good to other people who saw me drinking that day, so I picked hunters dry. We went to the bottle store, and he bought a carry pack and 2-750ml bottles of Smirnoff vodka which he was supposed to take to our relatives where there was going to be a ceremony the following day. My uncle paid and we went to the taxi rank where my cousin was waiting for us. We got in the taxi home and we started drinking our beers, and my cousin did not drink. My uncle was 26 years old back then and I did not call him uncle, I called him Ronnie. We were on our way home; I remember it was raining that day and we were enjoying our ciders. We did not finish them in the taxi because I remember when we got home to leave plastics, we still had 2 in the pack, and we also had one-one in hand. We then went to the tavern, and I was already feeling tipsy because that was one of my early days in drinking and I could not even drink properly. I would finish a 450ml bottle in 2 to 3 sips, I was rushing myself and nobody warned me. When we got to the tavern everybody was surprised to see me drinking because they had never seen me before. We played pool and jukebox and Ronnie bought more beers, and we changed to Castle 750ml. We were joined by his friends, and it was fun. It got dark around 7 pm and we were still drinking but I was already feeling that I was really drunk, so I sneaked out and left them. I went to church to try and look for girls, the was a night service that Friday and Saturday. I saw a girl that I had a crush on, and I hit on her right on the spot. Mind you I was drunk, and my nerves were not all over the place I was very persuasive, and she said we will finish our conversation the following day. We did not exchange numbers because she did not have a cellphone, girls' parents in the rural areas were very skeptical about buying their girl's phones and so I left without her phone number with the hope that I would see her the following day. I went home and slept and the next day when I woke up, I had a terrible headache, and someone said it was a hangover. I went to look for Ronnie in his room, but he was not there. I called him on his phone, and he said he was at our relatives where he was buying those 2 bottles of Smirnoff for. So, I went there and there was a traditional ceremony happening there. We call that ceremony Umombulo, it is when a widow is taking his/her mourning clothes off and they are about to go back to their normal life. I arrived and I found Ronnie and my other uncle. They were still very drunk because they did not sleep. We were a little distant from home, approximately 5kms and we walked there. We decided we should go home, Ronnie wanted to take a bath and get some sleep, so we walked me, him, and another uncle of mine who I also do not call uncle, I call him Joj. Those were the two guys that really got me started on the journey of drinking. We arrived home and Joj did not live with us, but he was our neighbor, so he went to his home. Ronnie slept and I stayed for a while and then I went out to get some air and I met the girl from the previous night, we talked, and she became my girlfriend. She was on her way to another night service; it was Saturday, and the service would start at 6 pm until 10 pm and some days even until 12pm. I told her that I was going to come to church at night to see her and she said it was okay. I went back home. It was still around 6 pm and Joj came. Apparently, they took one bottle to the relatives and stashed the other one, so Joj came with the other one. We started drinking and played some music in Ronnie's room. When the bottle was half Ronnie suggested that we should go to the tavern to get some beers and so we went. It was Saturday and it was packed it was also month end. People had money and we were joined by Ronnie's friends again; they were not really my friends at the time because I was young but, at those gatherings, we got along, and I considered them my friends too. We had fun and I got really drunk and sneaked out on them again. I left them and went to church again so that I could see my girl and that was a very bad decision because I was in a worse state than the previous night I was really drunk. I got to church, and I entered in the hall and walked to the back end where the youth sat. Our church hall is huge, and it was not full that day. The girl I had come to see, she saw me as I walked in that I was smashed beyond repairs. And I remember I would walk and pause, look around and start walking again. The destination was reached and there was no going back. I saw my girl and I went to seat right next to her. She could see I was really drunk and so could everybody else. There were even some elders who were seated where we were seated. I tried to make a conversation with her, but I was just mumbling she could not hear me "so she said" and this was getting attention because people were now staring at us. She knew I could get her in trouble because her grandmother was also there, so she moved away from me and changed the seats. I lifted my eyes and saw my ex-girlfriend seating next to her friend, the friend waved and said hi and I accepted the invite. I went and sat in-between them. I greeted them and then started to beg for love back from my ex-girlfriend. I was rough on her I called her a liar. I reminded her of all the promises she made and did not keep, I also told her friend some of the promises she made to me that she did not keep, and I remember she was very annoyed, but she did not change seats. I was very drunk, and everybody was watching all the drama that I was causing. Eventually, I blacked out and fell asleep. I put my elbows on my tights and my head above my tights. We were seated on a bench. I slept for a while and when I woke up, I started throwing up right on the floor. The 2 girls on either side of me jumped and ran away. I went on and on there was a huge dam of my vomit. Everybody was looking at me with large staring eyes, with one hand holding their mouth. My grandmom was also in the church, and she was a vice chairperson there. She sped up and came on the scene and she was very disappointed because she did not raise me that way. She ordered me right away to clean up my mess. I obeyed so I went outside to get some water and mop. I was accompanied by a friend Dez. He went to look for a dish and mop for me and we got some water from the tank. We carried the dish back inside together with the mop. When we got inside Dez offered to clean up the mess for me, but I refused him. I was not going to let my friend put himself in the position where he had carried a mess that was not his, something that I did on my own without anyone's help. First, I should not have been drunk like that in the first place and secondly, I was not supposed to go to church drunk and smell alcohol under any circumstances. Especially in a church where my grandmother's name was so big, the church she raised all her kids with, me included. I owned my mess; everybody was watching, and some were laughing at me. But I was too drunk to even think about them, I was busy minding my own business. I wiped out my vomit, as trying as that endeavor was, I remember I slipped on my vomit and my feet were twisting forward and backward but I held the balance with the mop, and I did not fall. I wiped out and left the spot without a tiny drop of vomit. I did leave some smell behind. After I had finished moping Dez offered to take the dirty water and mop outside, and I allowed him. At this time, I was so drunk, and I walked behind him. As I was walking, I turned around and looked at my ex-girlfriend and she was still staring at me with her hand in her mouth. I would walk and stop, look back and see her still staring and I could tell that was disappointment written on her face. I went home and got some sleep. On the following morning, I woke up and traced my steps by the church and I saw people were happy to see me. Even little kids were cheering me on, I was famous for all the wrong reasons. I was on my way to my older uncle's house to get my haircut and while I was there, having my hair cut by another guy I saw my ex-girlfriend walking parallel to me, but nobody said anything to anyone. I was not ashamed or anything, I was laughing at what I did myself, the only thunder I was afraid of was what my grandmother would say when she got back home late. After getting my haircut I went by the church and asked some girl to go and call my girl for me inside and she came, we sat outside all day. That victory, had I not got drunk the two previous days I would not have hit the girl when I did because she was a little younger than me, not that young I only left her by 2 years, but she had a twisted theory in her mind the previous years that I was old. It was now Sunday, I did not go back to school like I was supposed to, I went back Monday afternoon. I did not attend on Monday. Ronnie never went back to Cape Town like he was supposed to so I kept coming on weekends and we would get drunk, and I was now hooked. I was at a point where I really enjoyed drinking and getting drunk and it was one of those times where I told myself things like "I will never stop drinking" my grandmother was worried because she saw I was hooked on this thing, yet I had not even finished high school. I was doing grade 11 but I would come back home every weekend just to get drunk and never did anything productive at home like fixing the yard or anything. I was those times the brother would say I am enjoying life. I fell in love with drinking, and I remember in my drinking crew we recruited the tavern owner, we called him Geez. Now you can imagine how much we were now drinking with the tavern owner on our side. When I was now drinking officially and not those little experimenting things we used to do with my friends as kids, I never drank with the kids my age. I was drinking with older guys than me, some of who were old enough to be my father, the tavern owner for instance has kids about my age. I used to brag about the fact that I was drinking with older guys, and I would say to guys my age "I do not drink with kids I only drink with old fellows" and I was really proud of it. In my mind it made me look mature in the minds of other kids and I even thought that some of them probably thought I was better than them. I never had money to buy my own drinks those days my grandmother would not even give me money to buy groceries she would buy them for me and then give me some pocket money for school. I would save that money for a taxi to go home on weekends. When I got home it did not matter if I did not have any money, my older friends would buy drinks and we had the tavern owner as a part of our drinking crew. In my mind, I was living life. Some days we would drink all night. The tavern owner was our neighbor, and we are kind of related. When we were hungry at night we would go to his home. He would get tins of chakalaka and eggs which were stashed in his room he had a fridge there; we would make them and eat them with some bread. Sometimes he would even have red meat, Geez loved meat, we all did, and he still does. We would eat and finish the drinks we came with and then he would sleep. Ronnie and I would go home to sleep.

Alcohol slavery: My drinking got wild; I was at a point where I was doing what people call excessive drinking. And we were all hooked in that me and my guys. Ronnie and I started having fights when we were drunk, apparently, I was disrespecting him when once I got drunk, I thought he was just taking out his frustrations on me since he now had no money and did not go to Cape Town like he was supposed to. I remember this other Friday we were drinking, and it was raining, we were drunk he hit me, so I fought back. I was only 17 years old, and I was fighting with my 26-year-old uncle. The tavern owner got mad and picked Ronnie's side and they were now beating me together, a little strange for 2 older men ganging up on a kid. Geez whipped me with a sjambok on my legs and I fell down trying to cover up. They kicked me and they were stepping on my face like they were hitting some thug, mind you both these guys were my uncles. I lied down there, and I let them do their thing. After they were done, I woke up crying to myself and I went home to sleep. Ronnie came back at midnight and knocked on the door; we were sharing a room at that time I do not remember why. I opened it for him, and I went back to sleep. While I was sleeping, he hit me with a knobkerrie in the head and I bled. I woke up and grabbed the knobkerrie, we fought over it and I won it. I shoved him out of the way I did not want to hit him, I went to sleep with relatives. I knew then that I was a slave of alcohol. First of all, I should not have been drinking when I did not have money to buy my own drink. Secondly, I was very young to be caught up in that amount of alcohol consumption, and thirdly, I should not have been drinking with guys older than me, some even old enough to be my dad. I was way ahead of myself. When Ronnie and I were fighting at night my grandmother was in church, there was a night service, and she would sleep there when there was a night service. She had about the incident that had happened, so she came home on the following morning, it was Saturday. She called for my older uncle, and they intervened. They warned me against drinking, telling me that I was too young to be drinking alcohol and that I should focus on school. They warned Ronnie to stop feeding me alcohol. I do not know what was happening in the guy's head during that time. He was still threatening that he was still going to get me. I got tired of that, and I told him that I was not scared of him. He went out and got a tree butcher. He wanted to cut me with it, but my grandmother got in between us telling him to hit her. I knew right there that the guy was crazy, to pull a deadly weapon of that nature on his own nephew. My grandmother and older uncle decided I should go with my older uncle to his place that day because it was not safe for me to stay home, I would be left alone, and Ronnie would cut me with his tree butcher into slices. My grandmother was going back to church. I obeyed and I went with him. I did not drink on that day; I remember there was another Umombulo ceremony at a friend's home, they had slaughtered a cow and there was alcohol and he had invited me to come but I did not go. It was not because I did not want to go, I was wounded from the previous night's fight with Ronnie and Geez and from when Ronnie hit me with a knobkerrie in the head while I was sleeping. And besides that, I was going with my uncle to his place. My older uncle left me alone at his place and he attended the ceremony. I stayed there watching tv and sleeping all day. I also made some food in the evening. It was one of those days when you were content with sleeping and just being by yourself. I reflected at how lost I now was, how betrayed I felt, being beaten down like that by my own blood and a family relative, someone that I looked up to. I was so disappointed, and I could not even allow myself to take any of the blame. They were older, they should have known better, they would not beat their own kids like that, so why me, I was mad. I spent a night at my uncle's place. At night when my uncle had come back, in fact, he came back early in the evening at around 5 pm, when we were about to sleep, he gave me some words of wisdom and emphasized that I was a smart kid with a bright future ahead, I should focus on getting the education and stop drinking alcohol because it would destroy my life. I listened to my uncle, and it seemed like I heard him. On the following day, I went home to get my clothes so that I could bathe and go back to school, it was Sunday. I went back with bruises, one on my head and some on my legs. The ones on my legs were not a problem because they were covered by the trouser. I had to wear a hat school to cover the one in the head, it was not that bad, I just did not want to be annoyed by people asking me questions like, what happened. I stayed in town, and I did not go home for a few following weekends. I focused on my studies as my uncle said and I did well in my midyear exams. During midyear recess I went home, the dust had settled. Ronnie and I were cool, at least he was trying I did not shut him off. I do not hold grudges, not especially for my own blood. The other night I was coming back home from a friend, and I passed by Geez's home, his car was parked near the gate, and he was in it with Ronnie, he called me, and I came. They were drinking some savannas, he said he was sorry for what they did, and I said cool. He told me to get in the car and we went to his tavern to eat some meat. I remember I drank 3 savannas that night. We got back in the car and drove home, and when we got to the gate at his home we separated, Ronnie and I went home. I knew I was back to drinking and I did not even fight it. I did not even want to fight it because I really missed drinking, the only thing that was stopping me all this time is that I did not have my own money to buy myself alcohol. We started drinking together again and I was so happy to be reunited with my drinking crew. This time Geez and I got really close, I remember sometimes it would be just me and him and no Ronnie or anyone else. We would go to town together and I would help him to stock ciders and other stock items for his tavern. We would always braai some meat at the butchery whenever we were in town. The old drinking habits died hard. My grandmother saw that I was back to drinking and she warned me. I could tell she was sad; parents blame themselves when their kids are getting out of the way. I thought she was too serious, and she should chill. Geez, Ronnie and I would go to town to watch soccer tournaments on some weekends, we would drink later on and come back home drinking. Our friendship was now like never before, it was strong, and I felt really safe around these fellows. I thought they really loved me, and we all got along. This time I was no longer coming home every weekend just to drink, I would stay in town on some weekends and attend extra classes on Saturdays. On some other weekend, I would go home and still not drink. However, that behavior of having little control did not last me at all. In a very short while I was back to my old self. I remember when I am in school, I used to rush until it was the weekend so that I could go home. I was now missing to drink, I was now getting thirsty, at least that is an excuse we make when we want to get drunk. I remember in 2016 when I was doing matric, I was behaving like I was still in grade 2. I would leave school on Thursday and go home, and I would not attend on Friday. All this just to go and have some fun, at least that is what we said when we were getting drunk, we were getting fun. I would go back to school on Monday morning because I would still be drinking on Sunday. Sometimes I would not even leave on Monday morning, but I would go in the evening because I had drunk until it was very late on the previous night. My grandmother would fight me for this, and I could tell that if she was someone else, she would literally break down and cry. But she was very strong, I never saw my grandmother cry in my life. I was now at a point where I was officially a slave of alcohol, I was lying to myself and saying that I had it all under control. The truth is control is an illusion and it is a common attitude of all slaves of alcohol who do not want to accept that they are slaves to claim that they are in control. I was a slave of alcohol, and I could not control my own urge and that destroyed my life. Grade 12 students attended extra classes on weekends, and I was home drinking. During weekdays they went to school at 6 am and knocked off at 5 pm, I went to school at 8 am and I knocked off at 11 am because I would get bored in class. I remember this other Monday I was coming from home to school, we had drunk until I passed out on the previous night, I did not even know when I passed out, I woke up at 3 am and I was not even in my home I was at another guy's home that we were drinking with. As soon as I woke up, I went straight home, and I washed. I took my bag, and I went to the taxi stop. I was still feeling very drunk, and I had left school on Thursday, I did not even know what happens, so I had to go. I went to leave my clothes at my place, and I took my school bag and went to school. After the assembly we wrote a Math test in my class, apparently, students were informed on Friday to prepare for a test that was going to be written on Monday, but I was not there, so I did not prepare, let alone the fact that I was drunk. I could see Math a little and I knew that with practice I could be very good, but I never practiced. We wrote that test and I could not answer even a single question, my head would just spin around when I tried to think about the calculations. I tried but I could not solve anything, and I saw that the time was going, and I was not getting anywhere. I made another plan; I asked the guy who was seating next to me to show me his work to copy a few calculations so that I would not get zero and become the laughingstock of the class "not that I cared" and he showed me. I failed that test, and it was getting late, the year was moving, and it was now or never. I knew that it was now time for a change. I remember this other girl who was seating in front of me and we used to be friends, she was from my area, and she turned and asked why I was behaving the way I did, why was I not caring for my future and failing the subjects we both knew that I could pass without any trouble. Her words hit me; I knew my grandmother believed in me, but she did not know the things I was doing at school, so she never gave me those kinds of words. Now I had someone else who believed in my potential. On that day I left school again at 11 and went to my place but this time not to just sleep but to process things and think about my life. I now knew that I was a slave of alcohol because I was even bunking school and failing tests because of it. I made a decision that I would not go home on weekends, and I would read my books because I was very behind in all my subjects. That was the first productive choice I ever made that year. I decided that I would continue dodging classes and leave school at 11 am so that I could go and catch up on my own because I was very behind. Midyear exams had already passed which I failed excellently. We were now looking at trial exams. I studied by myself and committed to it. We wrote the exams and I failed them but this time I could see the positive change and it was a big change. I only failed Math and physics, so I knew I had to work to improve them. I did not aim high because I knew I was very behind I just worked hard not to fail them. The final exams came, and we wrote them. When we finished, I went home knowing that I did well, and I was not worried about anything. I celebrated that day, I met with my drinking fellows, and we got drunk.

Alcohol and self-destruction: self-destruction is defined as the behavior that causes serious harm to oneself. After finishing my matric in 2016 I went to Rustenburg, Northwest with one of my uncles the following year, in

2017. I went there to look for a job since I did not get accepted by any university then, in fact, I had only applied to Nelson Mandela University but my grade 11 report card which I had used to apply was not good enough. I was also not hoping that I would get accepted when I applied, I was just trying luck. When we got to Rustenburg, I posted my cv in a few places. I was a good kid in the beginning. During the day I would clean the room my uncle was renting which we shared. My uncle's name was uncle Themba. After cleaning the room, I would have some breakfast and watch tv. At 12pm I would start cooking so that when my uncle got back from work could eat. My uncle worked in the mines, he was in his early 30s when I was there, and we had drunk together before. On some weekends when uncle Themba was not working a few friends would visit, he would buy alcohol and we would braai some meat. At first, I did not drink I would watch them drink. There was another cousin of mine who lived in the same yard, and I used to hang out with him. We called my cousin Bodies, and he did not drink at all. Bodies and I would go out for some air to play pool and leave my uncle and his friends drinking. We would do that every time when my uncle had his friends around and we had done all that he wanted us to do for him. One day all my uncle's friends got drunk and left 6 beers in the fridge, it was castle lager my favorite back then. Late around 7 pm, I took one and I opened it. I finished it and opened the second one, I had this urge every time when my uncle and his friends were drinking but I was very shy to ask my uncle if I could join them. I was afraid that my uncle would deny me just to try and protect me. When I finally got a chance, my uncle was also there, my gulp was so big. It was like I had been thirsty for ages, "well, in the jargon we use when we are drinking, I was really thirsty for ages". I finished 3 beers alone in a very short time, a 750ml bottle, and then I went out alone. In my mind I was going out to look for girls, not that there were any my age where we lived and if there were any they were probably being locked out because I never saw them, in fact, I did because there was a high school there, but I think they saw anyone who was not going to school and was not working as some unworthy bastard. Anyway, as I went out alone, I got lost. We were living in a township called Sondela near the mines. Bodies and my uncle saw that it was getting late, and I had not come back yet so Bodies went looking for me and he found me. He got me home safe but what I did was the first sign of self-destructive behavior. In a city far away from home, in a township, I did not understand which had a history of violence and criminal activity. Uncle Themba did not yell at me or anything, we just laughed about it, and he warned me not to do it again. I listened to him, and I had won a fight I was afraid to fight, now every time uncle Themba's friends would come I would drink with them. I was back again to my old habits of drinking every weekend, I even made other friends and I would drink even if my uncle was not drinking. I forgot what it even was that I had gone there for, which was of course to look for a job. I got caught up in the life of drinking again and I saw my uncle was concerned. He would tell me to slow down but I believe it is easier to influence someone negatively than they can influence you positively. I remember uncle Themba was now drinking a little more than I knew him to do. I think he was comfortable that he now had his own nephew around and we could drink together. But I was still drinking a little more than he did because he would only drink on Fridays and Saturdays only and sometimes, he would drink only Saturdays. This was because he had to go to work on Mondays, so he did not drink on Sundays, and also, he was very responsible about his money. I would leave him on Sundays to continue drinking and this was getting a little out of hand, but I did not realize it at the time. I was addicted to getting drunk and being in places where people drank. During that time, I enjoyed watching generations the legacy, it had been my favorite show way before it was adapted to legacy. On the show, it was around the time when there were Russians who used Gaddafi Kumkani Phakade to distribute drugs and it was also during the time of Jack Mabaso and Ak's war. I fell in love with their art, but I think I might have fallen more in love with the idea of myself as a criminal kingpin. Because I remember this other day when I got so drunk and went to another club called Ebesuthwini, there was this other guy who was also drinking, he was moving his car to try and find the right spot to park. I asked him if I could get in, I had something I wanted to discuss with him, and he said "sure pop in" he looked gangster and I pitched a very stupid idea to him which I still find very stupid today when I think of it. I informed him that I wanted to open a drug operation and I wanted to recruit him. I have so much confidence when I speak especially when I am drunk, he must have believed me because we exchanged phone numbers. I was bragging about this to my cousin who was there to watch me to make sure that I was safe. I kept saying I was going to run the biggest criminal organization in the city. That was another self-destructive idea because it would not get me anywhere had

I implemented it. I would either end up dead or in prison. The following day I was sober, and I remembered what I had done on the previous day. I was ashamed because it was stupid enough to get in somebody's car that I did not even know and talk about selling drugs. What if he was a cop, what would I say? I allowed myself to be cool and forgive my stupidity but what I realized was that whenever I would be drinking that criminal mastermind idea would play in my mind like a movie. I started to believe that maybe that was my destiny, a very stupid thing anyone can believe about themselves. There was this other night, it was Sunday night, and I was watching fast and furious 7 on etv and I was drunk. My uncle was sleeping, at least I thought he was. My brother called, he lived in Joburg, and he is a pastor. He could tell that I was drunk, and I was also not keen to hide it. I told him right away that I was going to become the biggest drug lord in Rustenburg, and I was going to rule the criminal underworld. He tried everything to rebuke me the stupidity that was in my mind, but I did not care about any of that. I told him that this was my life and I had chosen what I wanted to do with it just like he did with his. He said okay because he could hear that I was not listening to him. He dropped the call and as soon as he did, I had a vision about stealing a car, and all this while I am under the influence of alcohol. I acknowledge that maybe these ideas were conditioned previously on me by tv, but I was now in a place where the energy was so high, and I picked up that energy also my emotions were high because of alcohol and so they fueled my thoughts. After that vision I took a bread knife from the table and went outside, there was a white BMW M2 Coupe that was parked outside our yard. I went to that car;

I slid the knife down the window trying to open the car, but I could not. That was very stupid, what if the owner saw me and shot me, what if the alarm went off. I went back inside, and I slept. What I did not realize was that my uncle saw me going out with a knife, and he asked me the following day if I was aspiring to be a criminal, that he saw me going out with a knife at night. I was ashamed and I denied it, even though he saw that I was not out of control. That was another very stupid and self-destructive move under the influence of alcohol. On the following weekend, me and my uncle drank on Friday and Saturday. Sunday my uncle did not drink so he went to watch soccer on the ground, and I went to drink. Late around 7 pm-8 pm, another lady approached me, and she gave me some money that she wanted me to pass to my uncle, it was R150, we were all drinking together with this lady. I used that money to buy more beers and that was another self-destructive move on the following day, the lady informed my uncle that she had given me money to pass to him. When my uncle got back from work, he saw me chilling with other guys by the place where I used to play pool. He called me to come saying he wanted to talk to me, I could sense there was trouble. I followed him and when we got to where we lived, he asked me about the money that was given to me to pass to him, and I told him that I used it to buy beers. He was very disappointed in me, and he told me to pay it with the money he had given me to go home, my uncle had given me R2000 so that I could go back home it was November and he would follow in December. I paid R150. I then went home on the following day and when I got there, I drank all the money I had left, it was R900 because I remember I used R600 for a taxi out of the

R1850 that was now left and when I got to Port St Johns, I bought a few things for R300, and I took a taxi to home. When I got home, I was reunited with Geez, the tavern owner. I would help him deliver cases of beer around the area to small shebeens. Another day Geez and I went to Mthatha, he wanted to stock some ciders. We went on the 22 December 2017, and we slept and came back on the following day. When we got to Mthatha I started drinking with Oskosh, another guy we were going to spend a night at his place. Geez did not drink on that day. I went out with Oskosh to another club called Bosase in Chrishani township. He bought beers and I sat and drank while he moved around and socialized. While I was seating down two guys came to me and started accusing me of stealing their beers, they were taking chances because they saw I was new there. But I was at my coolest, I just looked at them and drank my beer unintimidated. Oskosh saw what was happening and he came back and told these guys to back off, and that they would not handle me. They eventually did. I was then approached by a lady, she wanted me to have her phone number, she told me she was fascinated by how confident I was, and yet I was drunk. We drank our beers and finished them and then we left, the club was closing because beer was out. We went back to Oskosh's place. During that time, I had blacked out, I do not remember going. The next thing I remember is that I was surrounded by a gang of around 8 guys or so, I wanted to fight them. I told them to draw their knives if they wanted and that I was going to beat them, they drew their knives. My mind was seemingly coming back when they opened their knives and I told them to fold them back, and that we should not start what we could not finish. I do not understand until this day what was happening there, but it seemed like I was controlling what those guys were doing. I asked them to draw their knives again and this time the other guy was very angry. But lucky enough we were seen by Oskosh's friends who saw me with Oskosh, and they came to rescue me and took me back to Oskosh's place. I did not know what had gotten to me but when we got to Oskosh's place I slapped one of the guys who rescued me when he was telling a story of what had happened to Geez. Geez got angry and kicked me, he told me to go and sleep. A demon was now in control but that is the story for another chapter. I went inside and slept. On the following morning Geez told me what I had done, he said I went out by force after I had come back with Oskosh. He said that he tried to stop me, and he grabbed me, but I was too powerful, and I walked anyway. I did not even have the slightest idea of what he was talking about. How can someone blackout and still have the strength to do that, I knew I was in serious trouble, blacking out was not a new thing to me when I was drunk but I had never been told before that I had done something as stupid as what I did that night, something that nearly ended my life. That was a very self-destructive move. Anyway, Geez and I went to the city, and we stocked ciders and other items for his club and went home. In 2018 on the 23rd of February Geez asked me to accompany him to Mthatha again, we arrived at his nephew's place and the nephew had bought a bottle of Grants. We drank together first and when the bottle was about half, Geez was tempted to drink. After we finished that bottle, we went to Bosase club, Geez bought another bottle of Captain Morgan and some ciders. We were supposed to leave on the following day, but we ended up drinking all weekend. On Sunday morning we went to the city to buy more alcohol and meat and we came back to the township to have a braai. I did something very stupid again on that day. Oskosh and Geez went out to see some women leaving the car and the cars with the keys in the ignition. I started the car and got it out of the yard, and I drove. In my mind, I did not even know where I was going. I started pulling gear after gear, the last gear I remember pulling was gear number 5 in a very short distance. I saw Bosase club, and something flashed in my mind "where am I going" I hit the brakes while turning the steering wheel at the same time and I hit the car that was parked near the club, it was the club owner's car and I hit it very badly, an Audi A4. I knew I had destroyed my life. In a minute I was surrounded by the community, I got out of the car, Geez and Oskosh saw me, and they came running to rescue me so that I would not be beaten. The story is too long, I just wanted to show how destructive alcohol can influence a person.

Chapter 4- I was haunted by demons.

Psychology of demons: the psychology of humans is imperfect, and it can be twisted in many forms. That is why it can be easily manipulated. The foregoing statement was not adapted from any book or proved in any laboratory. It is something that I have observed in my own behavior as an individual living among other individuals whom I also believe that their psychology is as imperfect as mine. I believe that more than anything, our psychology is what makes us easy targets of slave masters. They come through this side of our being because they know it determines who we are and ultimately what we do. If you control a man's psychology, you control him and you can get him to do anything. Our psychology is shaped around what we believe. It can be constructive beliefs or destructive beliefs about ourselves. Constructive means that we accept positive beliefs about ourselves, and destructive means that we accept negative beliefs about ourselves. You can tell how a man thinks about himself or you can read his psychology by looking at how he conducts himself among fellow men. The beliefs we hold about ourselves and the environment shape our psychology. This is the most dangerous weapon an enemy can have against you. One should be very careful what beliefs he holds in his mind about himself, and also be careful not to let anyone use those beliefs against him in a process called reverse psychology. This is whereby another person makes you do something in a way that sounds like he is telling you not to do it and it is known to be very effective. The things we believe that shape our psychology is not only what people say or what we say to ourselves but also what we do. Our actions also shape our psychology. My experience with demons will prove the above statement.

I was once led into believing in the existence of demons and I found out by myself that they do exist. The way this happened is that I used to visit my father in Matatiele. My father believed in Sangomas (traditional healers) and this was new to me because where I grew up in Port St Johns my grandmother believed in God and she wanted nothing to do with Sangomas. What my father would do when I was there is that he would give me some of the traditional herbs he was using, and he would tell me that they would protect me from dark spirits. I had always heard about the existence of dark spirits when they preach in church but that did not have any effect on me at all. However, my father giving me those herbs was suggesting in my mind that there were demons after me and that I should protect myself from those demons. My mind accepted that suggestion when I took those herbs. Before that I did not really believe in the existence of any dark spirits, it was just a matter of hearing and maybe I would recall at night when it was dark, and I was walking alone, and it would make me scared. Now it was different, I was actually believing that there are demons after me. Every time I took or used any of those herbs I was strengthening and intensifying that belief and I succeeded in that because it got to a point where I believed that I was all-powerful and invincible. I remember when I was drunk, I would go around saying "Andikhothwa silwane sagqwirha mna" which is Xhosa meaning "no demons of witches can touch me" I was now calling for disaster because I was no longer intensifying the belief only by using herbs, but I now had an affirmation too, an affirmation that I used when I was drunk when I had consumed one of the most powerful brain stimulants. That went on and on until it became who I was. I believed in myself that I was that person, and I would not be touched by demons. The subconscious mind, however, took the belief that I believed there were demons after me, and it acted upon it accordingly. I want to repeat this statement, by accepting the traditional herbs from my father, I was agreeing that there was a demon after me, when I started using the herbs, I was creating a belief in my mind that there really was a demon after me, by using the herbs over and over I was intensifying that belief. What followed was that in 2017 when I was in Rustenburg with my traditional herbs with me, which I was using every day. In May of that year, my aunt back home died, and we had to go home to bury her. 2 days before my aunt's funeral another cousin of mine was haunted by a demon we did not understand. As that invincible guy I was I took out my trusted herbs and made a mix for him to drink and I sprinkled some around the house and around the yard, chasing and casting demons was the affirmation at that time, I was now a little Sangoma myself. This seemed to have helped him on the first night because we slept, but on the following day which was a day before the funeral he worse, we could not tell what was going on with the fellow. I mixed my herbs again and sprinkled them around, he came back late, he had run away and when he came back, he seemed fine. Anyway, I went back after the funeral to Rustenburg with my uncles, it was on Sunday when we left. On Thursday during that week, I was at the gymnasium, and what happened is that my eyes started jumping, I was seeing burred visions of nothing that kept popping up and down in my eyes. I panicked because I had never had anything like this before and it was scary. I stood there for a while thinking that it would stop but it was only getting worse. I took my bag which had my changing clothes in it, and I carried it, I could not change because I was now not seeing anything, all I could now see were those blurred visions of nothing that kept popping up in my eyes and they were getting faster every second. During this time, I was no longer seeing anything. I was using my memory to find my way which was also disturbed because what was happening induced a lot of fear in me. After all that panic, I blacked out. When I woke up, I was surrounded by people and my uncles were there to pick me up. The people who saw me said I jumped and fell, and I started having a seizure which was something I never had in my life before. I had a very terrible headache when I woke up on my left side of the eye. My uncle called my uncle and informed him about what happened, and my father told him that I should come home his brother who is a Sangoma was back from cape town for a while. I went on the following day. In western culture, they call your father's brother an uncle so I will do the same here to simplify matters. When I got to Matatiele my uncle consulted the ancestors and they informed us that some 3 ladies after the funeral we were attending of my aunt, went above the grave stabbed knives calling my name and saying they will be the ones who will finish. This caught my attention and my conscious belief about a demon haunting me was now stronger than before because I had seen the signs, in my mind, it did not occur to me that what was happening was a result of that stupid belief. My uncle recommended a small ritual that my father had to perform with me, and he gave me more herbs that I had to use, and I would take them with me to Rustenburg. We performed the ritual and that kept me going for some time and I was fine until I was not. I kept recalling what had happened to me and I was afraid of it happening again. After 2 months after we had performed the ritual and I was back in Rustenburg, my uncle and his wife left me alone in the room they were renting to go to visit some relatives in Germiston and they would come back late. The blurred visions started, and I got scared and started shaking, it was seemingly getting serious, but I realized I was alone, so I closed the door and sat on the chair, and I looked straight forward. To my surprise, the visions just faded. I did not know they were not serious, or that I defeated them. I informed my uncle and his wife when they got back about what had happened. The following day we went to see another Sangoma in the area, he consulted with the ancestors, and he told us something completely different from what my father's brother had told me, I thought he was crazy, I thought the demon was crazy, it was driving me to different Sangomas knowing that they would tell me different theories that did not make any sense. I did not say anything I just listened to whatever madness that Sangoma was telling us, and he recommended we to perform the same ritual we had already done with my father. I could not understand whether his ancestors could not tell him that what he was telling me to do I had already done, or maybe he was a con artist, and it was his game to play with people's hopes. I thought he was very cruel. We eventually left and along the way, I informed my uncle that none of what that guy had said made any sense and it never happened to me and that I was not going to perform his stupid ritual because it was something I had already done, and it did not work. My uncle understood and we went to the flat. After that, I was fine for a while until on the 22nd of December 2017 when I went with Geez to Mthatha. When I was at Bosase club with Oskosh and he left me seating and drinking while he was moving around and socializing, the blurred visions started. I was now between more than 50 people in a club who were drunk, it would be very embarrassing to have a seizure. I applied the same attitude I did in Rustenburg when I was all by myself. I took a sip of my beer, and I looked straight forward, and it stopped. I defeated it again for the second time, but I still could not tell how. I also believe that the demon had something to do with me blacking out and finding myself surrounded by men with knives. The following day after we finished stocking in the city Geez and I went back to Chrishani to get the pork he had come to cut; we had left it there in the fridge when we went into the city. When we were by the house where we left the pork, the blurred visions started. They caught me off guard and I panicked. My body got cold very fast. I could feel myself losing power and I started seeing my dead family members in the blurred visions. I remember saying to Geez here is my family. I had another seizure and blacked out. When I woke up, I started throwing up and I did not even have the strength to stand. I was very weak, and they gave me some water to drink and wash. We got in the car and drove home. In January 2018 I went to Matatiele again to see my father's brother. He consulted with the ancestors again and we performed another ritual with him this time and it was different from the one we had performed before. I was so convinced that it would work and then I went back to Port St Johns. On 2 April 2018, I was visiting some relatives to see a cousin who was sick. When I got there the visions started, I tried so hard to apply the same attitude I had defeated them with before, but this time I did not succeed, I was overwhelmed, and I suffered another seizure the third one this time. I realized that none of those rituals I was performing and the traditional herbs I was using were doing me any good. In the following week, I was walking home, and I met, and I met a Sangoma who was visiting another home in the area. He stopped me and asked who I was, and I told him my name. He told me that he could see that I was haunted by demons. I was surprised, that someone I had never seen before told me something like that, something that I was battling with. He told me where he was going, and we separated. I went home, I knew my grandmother wanted nothing to do with Sangomas, so I did not bother saying anything. on the following morning I was going out to search for some goats which my uncle had recently bought and were now lost. When I was approximately 3kms away from home the visions started, I panicked because I saw that they were getting strong, and I walked very fast so that I could get home before anything happened. It was getting intense. As I was walking home, I saw the Sangoma from the previous day, he was at a distance, and we were coming toward each other. The first thing that hit me was joy and it replaced the fear that was boiling inside me. The visions just vanished; I could not tell what had just happened but out of joy I informed the Sangoma. He told me to go and get his numbers from the home he visited so that I could call him. I told myself I would not do that because my grandmother would not want him in her house, and secondly, I did not have the money to pay him. All this time this was happening in 2018 I had a girlfriend in Cape Town that I met on Facebook, and we were now chatting even on WhatsApp. Our relationship was heating up and I knew I was in love. I promised my girl that I was going to see her and that I was going to see her in the year 2018. I vowed to her that I was going to see her in Cape Town, and she believed in me. I informed my grandmother that I wanted to go to Cape Town to look for a job, she asked what about this thing that was haunting me. I told her that I would not stay at home and do nothing because I was afraid of what might happen, I told her I was going and that whatever happened I would deal with it when it did. My grandmother arranged and I went to Cape Town on the 05th of June 2018. I was healed completely until today; I never had those blurred visions and seizures. That is why even today I still believe, and I will always believe that my grandmother and my girlfriend Zoe are my angels. The desire to see my girl and to be with her gave me the courage to face my demons. I was willing to risk it all and go to Cape Town just to see her. My grandmother's question to me about the demons that were haunting me and my response to it induced me to make a firm conviction to myself that I was going forward, and nothing could stop me. I won the fight against the demons even though I was now not consciously engaged in it. I believe this story will put things into perspective about a lot of things on the passage about psychology. It literally proves that not only words can strengthen a belief, but actions are suggestive, and they strengthen a belief as well. A negative idea that has been accepted as the truth and believed can cause serious damage to an individual's psychology and ultimately in his life. I hope this story changes your life.

Chapter 5- how I got scammed.

Scamming and Marketing: scamming means committing a fraudulent or deceptive act or operation, for example, an insurance scam. The way a scam works involves an element of marketing. The scammer pitches an idea to the victim and the victim buys that idea and loses his/her money. Of course, scamming involves a lot of other things it is not only limited to money but for the purpose of this book, I will talk about money scams. As an individual, I have hopes and dreams. Our society is designed so that we always want more. This is good as I have said in the previous chapter that greediness is a necessary emotion. But the way scammers work is that they promise you your hopes and dreams and you buy to that. Recently I was a victim of an online scam. I was going through a tough breakup with my partner of four years. I saw a good-looking lady on Facebook who posted photos of her and her kids living it large in the UK, London. She also posted some motivational messages on her timeline which is what interested me. I viewed her profile and I saw that she listed she was from Nyanga, Cape Town, South Africa. I was astonished by how a young South African, a female to say, ended up in the life she was living. Mind you, I was going through a breakup so seeing her posts and the fact that she was from Nyanga, a very notorious township in Cape Town gave me hope. I started thinking that somewhere out there, there was something waiting for me to do, someone waiting to be paired with me. I commented on one of her posts, it was nothing lengthy or desperate, I wrote a single word "inspirational" and after that, I did not know what happened. A message popped in my inbox saying "hi", and I said hello. She introduced herself and I did the same. She wanted to know where I lived and what I was doing, of course, to ask me those questions she would have to tell me about herself first. She told me she was from Nyanga, and she was now living in the UK, she said she was working for an offshore diamond drilling company and that she was the assistant and special advisor to the manager. I did not want to ask any penetrating questions. I told her that I was living in Port Elizabeth, and I was a university student, I also told her that I was going to Nelson Mandela University which was the only university that carries Madiba's name in South Africa or all over the world, something that I always brag about, I never leave that detail out when I am asked which university I am going to. She was glad to know me, and I was glad to know her. She proceeded to ask if we could be friends and that she enjoyed talking to me. I said sure, I mean what came to my mind at that time was that maybe she misses home, and talking to someone back home would kind of fill the gap even though I was sure that she communicates with her family back in Nyanga. She then asked that we live chat on the webcam. I did not even know what that was, and she said it was an iPhone or Apple laptop app where people can video call. I told her that I did not own any apple cell phone or laptop. She asked why and proceeded to tell me that in a country like ours where there was a poor connection service everyone needed to have an apple laptop or as she puts it "needed to get their hands on an apple laptop" and that it was imperative that I get one as soon as possible. To me she was starting to sound like a spoilt brat, that to me represented an attitude of a rich person who knew nothing about being poor except for what they saw in the newspapers, if she even read the newspapers, she was very insensitive. I told her that I did not have the money to buy apple products and that I had a dell laptop and a Hisense brand cellphone, and they were servicing me just fine. She asked if apple products were too expensive in our country, and I told her they were. She told me I should get them by all means and that irritated me a little bit because she was now telling me what I should do yet she did not even know me or my struggle. But I did not show in our conversation that I was getting annoyed by what she was saying, I told her that I did not have rich parents and that even my education was paid for by Nsfas. We changed the conversation for a while and she asked me how did I feel about meeting people from overseas I told her that I did not have any fantasies about how other people lived in their countries and that there was one life, it did not matter from which part of the world you came from, you still breathe the same oxygen that I breathe and get the same 24hours that I get per day, I also told her that I was all about reading the energy and I could tell everything I wanted to know about a person by reading their energy. She was impressed but I was not trying to impress her, I just did not want her to think that I was some sort of a groupie or anything like that. She then said she would like to be my close friend and communicate every time we can, I said sure. This lifted my hope up because I was now going to be friends with a successful person who also happened to be living and working abroad. All I could think of was how much I was going to learn from her and that I was worth something despite what the girl I had broken up with a thought about me. I thought that God saw that I was going through pain because of losing my girlfriend and now she brought this girl into my life to console me and make me realize my potential. For a while, I forgot about the breakup and focused on that moment. At that moment I was not thinking about anything else that could possibly go wrong, my thoughts were turned inwards, I was thinking that the universe was finally responding to my prayers and struggle. She proceeded to ask me that, if she could buy me an apple laptop and would I be able to receive it because she really enjoyed chatting with me and she liked to chat on the webcam and that she would love to have me there. I could not believe what she had just said to me, I mean I had just become friends with a very beautiful and successful woman who lived and worked abroad and now she was offering to buy me a laptop with her own money. What I felt inside was no longer just hope, my heart was pounding in an unusual way it was jumping, and I think I fell in love with her at that moment. I would view her photos on her profile and say to myself "God I do not know what I did to deserve this, but whatever it was that I did, I was glad that I did it" I responded to her and said "yes" I would be able to receive it because there was an airport in the city where I lived. She informed me that on the following day after she had finished her work, she would go to the electronics store to buy it and that she was going to take a picture of the laptop for me so that I could see if I liked it and I said okay. Of course, beggars cannot be choosers, "are you kidding me" I already loved it even though I had not seen it yet. On the following day around 4 pm here in South African time she texted, and I was on high alert, I replied very quickly. She sent a photo of the laptop and asked if I liked it and I said I loved it. She asked if I would also like for her to buy me an iPhone. I said if it would not be a problem with her, I would love it, and that it was even more portable than a laptop. She showed me a photo of the iPhone too and told me that she was going to make a payment for the items we would talk about when she was done. Now I had seen the items and I was so happy, my heart was now pounding even faster than before, I remember that I even saved some pictures of her, and I went to post one on my WhatsApp status and I captioned it "goddess". She texted again saying she was done making payments and that she was now going to the airport to have them forwarded to me. I said okay. Late around 8 pm she texted "dear" I said "hello" and she told me she had forwarded the items and that when she got to the embassy, she was informed that the only plane to Africa which was left that night was going to Nigeria. I panicked because first of all, I had never delivered or had anything delivered to me by flight courier before and secondly, I did not live in Nigeria I lived in South Africa and I had never been in any other country than my own country, I did not even have a passport, so how was the hell was she expecting me to receive those items. She told me that she was left with no choice but to deliver the items via Nigeria and that she was still driving at that time she was going to send me a document I would need to receive the items when she got home and the instructions, she was given which I had to follow in order to receive the items.

That seemed to have relieved my stress. She then texted again, later on, this time she forwarded a document that looked like a receipt/slip which she said I would have to provide in order to receive the items and it looked legit. I could see her name was written as the sender and I was mentioned as the receiver. I was now more believing than before. On that same slip, she gave me there was a Nigerian phone number which she said she was told at the embassy that I would have to call and get instructions about receiving my items. The number was listed as the customer officer number. I could not sleep that night and so I rose up from bed and sat on my chair, I watched music on YouTube with my laptop all night. Music is another thing that fuels emotions, at this point, I was not thinking straight. My mind was fixated on the idea that I was going to have an iPhone and Apple laptop and I was going to take a photo of them when they arrived and post it on social media and show t the people that God really works in mysterious ways. In the morning I called the number, I made my first call at 5 am, I could not wait, an early bird catches the fattest worm. But no one picked up and I assumed that since it was an office it would open maybe around 8 am to 9 am although I did not know Nigerian working hours. When I first called, however, I was under the impression that since it was an airport and it operated 24 hours the office would pick up. But I was very early anyway because I was informed that the items would arrive at 6 am. I called again at 6 am, still no answer, I went to google to search Nigerian time and I found that they were behind us by an hour and so I waited. I called again at 9 am and a man picked up. I told him my name and that I was calling about my items which were supposed to arrive there at 6 am, and that it was a transshipment, they had to forward them to South Africa. He asked what my customer number was. On the slip, they had written 452 and the lady had emphasized that and so I gave it to him. He informed me that my items had arrived. I asked him how I was going to get them, and he told me that I would have to apply for their delivery service. I asked him how do I apply, he told me that I had to go to their WhatsApp channel and apply there. I then asked him to give me their WhatsApp number and he told me that it was the same number I was calling him from. I dropped the call and went straight to WhatsApp. I gave him my customer number again on WhatsApp and he asked me to forward him the document I had been given which I was informed that I would have to provide in order to get the items, I forwarded it. He asked for my address, and I gave it to him. He gave me a Capitec account number and told me that I had to deposit R2000 South African currency on that account. I did not even go to google to ask to convert R2000 into Nigerian currency, I just asked him after I had deposited the money, how long would it take for me to receive the items and he told me before nightfall on that day. That was something I find very stupid even today because it was on a Saturday and Nigeria is another country, it takes 3-7 days to deliver around South Africa, how was I expecting items from another country to arrive so quickly. I said okay, I informed my roommate that I was going to the bank to withdraw R2000 and I was going to deposit it, I had items that I needed to get from Nigeria. At this time, I was bragging to him and acting all important. I then went to the bank and withdrew the money and deposited it at the same time. I took a picture of the slip and forwarded it on WhatsApp and the guy informed me that they confirmed my payment. I asked what was going to happen now and he told me to wait and that they would be in touch. I informed the lady who had forwarded me the items that I had just paid for them, and I was now waiting to receive them. It seemed like she was happier than I was, and I did not know why. If I already knew then that it was a scam, I would have said she was celebrating. She told me that she had also put 900 pounds in the laptop so that I could recover the money and that she was informed that I would have to pay (a detail she had left out before). I did not see through it that it was all just a scam at the time. I went to google and converted 900 pounds into Rands, and it converted to 18k. this lifted my spirit, I could now imagine the things that I was going to do with 18k, I was even going to make a driver's license and prove to my family that I could do something for myself, I was going to prove to myself that there was something special about me and that for some reason God favored me more than them, I was going to prove to the girl that I had broken up with that I was worth something and that all along she had been blocking my shine and now that she was gone things were now clearing up for me. How wrong and foolish I was to just put my trust out there like that. After I had deposited the money, I went back to my room and waited. The guy texted again "sir" I replied "hello" he told me that when they were filing my items, he realized that I also did not pay the LDC and when I went to google, I found that it was a fee that least developed countries had to also pay when using flight courier. The first question in my mind was that I gave him the document long ago and it was written on the document that I had not paid that fee, why was he only telling me that now? I asked him how much I had to pay even though I had seen it on the document, and he said it was $150 US dollars. I went to convert on google and it converted to R2224 at the time. I asked him how much would it cost in rands even though I had seen it for myself. He went through the same process as I did and he also took a screenshot, at this time I am watching his enthusiasm. I asked him how I was supposed to pay the money and he said "kindly deposit the money to the same account sir" I thought he was crazy because from that moment my mind went to speed, and everything cleared. The hopes went down, and the wisdom of ages came to my rescue. Everything that had just happened played in my mind like a movie and I knew then on that I had fallen for a scam. I was seating on my chair when the movie played in my mind, and I chuckled first then drank some water. I took my clothes off and got in bed, for the first time in my life I had fallen for a scam, and I knew I was dealing with professionals. Well, they were not really professionals otherwise I would not have seen through their scam. I responded like a fool and said I would not be able to come up with that amount of money, I did not have it in my account. The stupid lowlife thug asked how much I had they would give me a discount and that confirmed everything, an airport giving discounts. I called the lowest number and said I had R300, I think he felt sorry for me because if he did not, he would have asked for it, it seemed to me like he was trying to squeeze me for every penny he could get from me. He then said "do not worry sir you will get the money, your items will be safe until you get the money" I wanted to insult him for his stupidity, that he did not realize that I was now seeing through their stupid scam, but I held it together and told that I did not think I would manage, and I asked for a refund instead. He politely informed me that they did not do refunds. I said to myself "I forgive myself for having a weak side and I forgive these guys for being cruel". I then went to Facebook to inform my new friend who had supposedly forwarded me the items. I wish I could say I was surprised to see how keenly she was that I pay for the items, she was no longer just a friend, she was now calling me babe, she confessed her feelings for me and told me that they were the reason she even bought me those items. And all that just to get me to give them more of my money. From that moment on I was very objective. I did not care about anything I just enjoyed playing a game of logic with her. I knew I could not get my money back my supposed customer officer had at least informed me of that in a very polite way. But I also knew something else which I was going to use to my advantage during that whole conversation. First, I had seen through the scam that she was part of (if she was even a girl) and she did not know that, secondly, I knew that she was never going to get another penny from me and she did not know that I had an edge. Since they had defeated me in the first round and got away with my money, I was going to defeat them in the second round. My strategy or game plan was easy, firstly, I was going to make them see that I was not broken, and I did that by not insulting or complaining, secondly, everything she was going to say to try to make me give them more money I was going to counteract that with unquestionable logic why I was not going to do it. She kept stressing about the 900 pounds she claimed she had put on the items and how it would help me recover the money. But unfortunately, this time her promises were no good. I acknowledge that even though I might have been greedy in that entire situation, most of it was a result of hope. I was in a very dark place, and I needed hope to this day even though the situation turned out to be a scam it gave me the hope that I needed. I lived in the fantasy world for some time, and I paid dearly. But what happened here, ladies and gentlemen. Materiel things which I associate with marketing because they come to us, or we learn about them through marketing are important in our lives. And because they are important, cruel people use them to manipulate us. In hopeless situations spoiling yourself might lift up your spirit. My situation was exactly that way, I was in a hopeless situation and my spirit needed lifting. What I did however was gambling by definition, I substituted a game of hope for a hopeless situation. Most men who gamble are driven by greed, and as much as I was in a vulnerable situation at the time, there was an element of greediness in the story. I was not conscious of my greediness throughout the entire time until the time when I wanted to blame someone. I want to agree that when I commented on the lady I wanted her recognition because I was charmed by her success. This was because my whole life I had been chasing success which I call chasing a fantasy. Seeing that lady on my list of friends, and commenting on her posts seemed like the next right thing to do because she was the person already living the life that I wanted to live if not more. I was not at fault; I do not walk around consciously aware of every process or mechanism that is currently taking place in my mind or body. I needed hope but I could not find it within, I also did not seek it through material stuff, but it was suggested to me by an outside source through material stuff. Of course, I am human I also expect outside stimuli to give me answers that I seek within. So, I accepted an idea without analyzing it because I was emotional and vulnerable. This is what scammers like in their victims, they target vulnerable people because their game is a game of hope. They are selling hoping. Besides vulnerable people they also target greedy people, they advertise to them their desires knowing it would make their hearts soft and so paralyze their minds. Be careful, the world is full of people who are just out to make money, they do not care at what cost